THERE IS AN 'F' IN HURLING

AIDAN LENEHAN

Ballpoint Press

ABOUT THE AUTHOR

Aidan Lenehan is a Galway man. Born in Galway City, he spent most of his early years in East Galway. It was in Kiltormer that he first discovered hurling.

He played for the club for eight years before transferring to Padraig Pearses in south Roscommon. In 1989 he moved to the capital, where he has been ever since. That move coincided with his hurling career going into gradual pause. He made his return to competitive action with the Wild Geese in 2008, 16 years after his retirement.

He now lives in Rolestown, North County Dublin with his wife Joan and son Michael.

ABOUT THE GHOSTWRITER

Rory Kerr is from Raheny on the north side of Dublin. He studied journalism in Colaiste Dhulaigh, College of Further Education. He has been writing on GAA games since 1990. Today he works as the GAA Correspondent with the Fingal Independent.

*To my son Michael
and wife Joan*

Published in 2012 by Ballpoint Press
4 Wyndham Park, Bray, Co Wicklow, Republic of Ireland.
Telephone: 086 8217631
Email: ballpointpress1@gmail.com

ISBN 978-0-9572072-1-9

Book design and production by Elly Design

Printed and bound by GraphyCems

CONTENTS

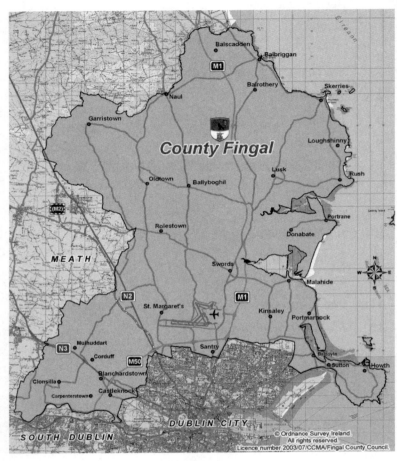

Ordnance Survey *Ireland*

National Mapping Agency
www.osi.ie

ACKNOWLEDGEMENTS

I would like to thank the lads, every one of them for their encouragement and openness, allowing me to portray us 'warts and all'. This is your GAA footprint, it will never be forgotten.

In life one occasionally meets great people. People that make a difference, the 'is feidir linn' generation. Well PJ Cunningham, you're one of them. Thanks for believing in me.

At the beginning of this journey, I was just a lad with a tale to tell, but I knew my writing would need fine-tuning. That's where Rory Kerr came in. A wordsmith with empathy and patience. Good to work with you.

A special mention to Ger Loughnane, a living legend, who encompasses all that's great about hurling. Thanks Ger for your assistance and wise words.

Many thanks to the president of the GAA, Liam O'Neill for sharing his time so generously.

They say a picture tells a thousand words and photographer Paul Connell kindly gave me literally hundreds of great images to choose from that he had snapped over the years. If you need a good photographer, he's the man.

Many thanks also to Susan Flatley for the use of her images.

I would like to particularly thank John Costello, the Dublin County Board, Sean Flatley, Ed Sweetman, Peter Dunphy, Dave Sammon and the Wild Geese committee, Tony and Patsy Hough, Daniel O'Connell and the team in OSI.

I will always hold a special debt of gratitude to Frank Curley, who quit as manager of the 1982 Galway senior champions to concentrate on juvenile hurling in Kiltormer. My hurling became a by-product of his efforts. John Molloy further nurtured this during my Garbally years.

This book is a dream come true for me. I love books, that love was ignited during my Garbally years, where I learnt some other things as well as hurling. Special mention to Mick Lally and Joe Molloy.

I would especially like to thank my parents PJ and Phil, brother Fergal, sisters Helen and Fidelma. I have been blessed to have a remarkable family. We do not see each other that often, that's down to geography but when we do, we just take up where we left off.

I started the last decade with my closest childhood friend, Justin Noone being laid to rest on my 30th birthday. The same decade ended with my brother-in-law, Dave Carvill passing away suddenly. Life is short. The person, who has shown me this and taught me to embrace it, is my wife Joan. One of her favourite sayings is 'you're only around the block once' and I am lucky she's with me as I travel it.

My son Michael is the most amazing thing that ever happened to me. I hope you'll enjoy reading this.

Go raibh maith agaibh go léir.

FOREWORD

For me, the Ireland of today is a complex and paradoxical country; its residents equally so. It seems we spent hundreds of years trying to rid ourselves of the shackles imposed upon us by foreign powers, only for most of us to embrace globalisation unconsciously even before the first centenary of our freedom.

We are on the path to losing our Irishness. Almost one hundred years ago both my grandfathers were there when our country was born. One risked the wrath of 'The Black and Tans' in Roscommon to play his beloved Gaelic football. The other witnessed first-hand the Dublin 'lock out', the 1916 rising and mixed with the IRB leadership, one of the architects of a free Ireland. Neither were extreme nationalists but both were proud to be Irish. One of the best expressions of Irishness is hurling.

A unique and truly skilful Irish game.

This is an authentic tale of a humble effort at a hurling renaissance. The characters in this true story come from all walks of life. The book charts their efforts at playing this amazing game from early stages of a newly-formed team in 2008 until the 2012 season. For most, it was their first time. There were many ups and downs along the road. To win can be easy but to preserve the fruits can be difficult. There have been many disagreements, flaws, transfers but against the odds, we have managed to survive and maintain our strong bond of friendship throughout and enjoy ourselves on the way. The idealism we started with has been dented but not diluted.

This is a story of courage.

The epicentre in this story is Oldtown. In the Pale, certainly. But it's not what most envisage as 'Dublin'. It's a tiny village a few fields away from the Meath border. It's nestled in the centre of rural North West Fingal. The area has seen much strife before this raggle-taggle bunch of hurlers. This land has witnessed confederate battles and the last stand of the Wexford 1798 pike men. The locals are fiercely proud and immediately saw the opportunity hurling gave them to help re-establish their dormant GAA club. That we have representation from eight neighbouring Gaelic football clubs in the hurling teams first outing, highlights the togetherness and sense of community we have achieved. All inter-club rivalries were paused. We succeeded in sowing the hurling seed in a once barren region.

This is not just a book about hurling. Ireland's landscape has changed drastically during the story. We see the loss of our financial sovereignty and the beginning of a recession. We have gone from full employment to high levels of unemployment in a very short time. The spectre of 'no work' has taken a grip and the haunting presence of emigration comes over us. We have lost many pillars of the community.

History repeats itself with many of our Wild Geese having had to take the route of the original Wild Geese. Both had little choice.

Regardless, every week thousands of men and women take to the GAA fields to play their sports. Through thick and thin they carry the mantle with pride. Most play at junior and intermediate levels. The real grassroots level and while this is our story, it's also their story.

Bain sult as an scéal.

CHAPTER 1
THE ONE TRUE FAITH

It was on a summer's evening in 2009 shortly before highlights of the Munster hurling final were due to be shown that Sean 'Flats' Flatley, the Wild Geese goalkeeper, spoke these memorable words to the nation as they sat down to their weekly helping of The Sunday Game

'We've played 23, won one, drew one and lost 21 so I think this year, there is plenty of room for improvement'.

In that one short pithy sentence we had been laid bare for all to see – and yet we had arrived.

We are a small club in a rural north County Dublin, in a village called Oldtown. We had been selected out of hundreds of teams to receive a once-off training session from Clare legend, Ger Loughnane.

When the Sunday Game producers rang Ger Loughnane briefing him on our status his reaction was 'Junior E! You must be joking'. It was unheard of down in most parts of the country to have a championship that low and the great man must have been wondering what he had let himself in for.

Still by stepping inside the St Mary's sports grounds, he had along with Oldtown's most famous resident Molly Weston (she along with her two brothers was to lose her life at the Battle of Tara 1798) helped put this remote rural village on the map once more.

It would be a lie to say Loughnane's visit changed our fortunes but what it validated was our struggle to keep hurling alive in a small village of 300.

As it happened, a few seasons later we were to drop down a grade after he left and while we were loathe to admit there was an 'F' in hurling, this is where we are at the time of putting this book together.

We have been together four years now as a team, our players having come from many clubs in North County Dublin.

There have been 'tears' along the way, sliotars have been lost, hurls have broken, players have left, or through the course of work or in search of a better future, have moved on.

Through all this, the team has stayed together, one of the reasons being to give an outlet for our juveniles when they came of age.

It was then with some personal satisfaction that on August, Sunday 19th, 2012, 16-year-old Fionn Andrews, son of experienced inter-county manager, Val, became the first player from our hurling academy to make his senior debut.

After a turbulent few years the future was looking rosy once more and yet it might never have happened had it not been for a chance school reunion back home in Galway.

This is where the story of the Wild Geese hurlers begins, about a bunch of lads, most of whom never played the game before. Those who had were considered over the hill but persevered against the odds, in a hurling wasteland to not only start a team but survive for five seasons. This is their story.

CHAPTER 2
THE SPARK

It was at a school GAA reunion organised by my former hurling mentor John Molloy in 2006 that I rediscovered my love for hurling.

Many giants of the game had perfected their skills at St. Joseph's, Garbally College, Ballinasloe. All Stars Sean Silke, Iggy Clarke, Ollie Kilkenny, Michael Duignan, Conor Hayes were a sample of the calibre of hurling talent that passed through the school corridors.

I had five happy hurling years there as well as receiving a good education. I then moved to Dublin, where I did a year in the D.I.T. It was not for me, so I started working full-time and with that my involvement in hurling slowly evaporated.

The reunion was attended by GAA president, Nicky Brennan, and I met many former school mates most of whom I had not seen in two decades.

I was astounded that many, even of my vintage and older, were still playing competitive hurling. Most had never stopped.

So I was quietly envious and that turned to regret. During my days in this hurling wilderness I had spent my free time on the golfing fairways but soon that turned into a chore. I had reached my mid-life crisis and my idleness on the couch had not gone unnoticed by my wife Joan.

I was getting 'under her feet' and by means of a gentle push she suggested I consider taking up a hobby.

But it was at the reunion that the concept of a comeback was well and truly planted. You only live once and I was not prepared to let this chance slip again.

In my early years as a hurler I was something of a late bloomer. But patience and practice served me well and I eventually made it on to the Kiltormer team that won the Galway under-16 county in 1986. In 1988 my family moved to Creagh, pronounced like 'Korea', situated on the Roscommon side of Ballinasloe where I was to transfer to Padraig

Pearse's. Not such a retrograde step in those days. Roscommon clubs had won three Connacht senior hurling titles in the previous decade and that was during Galway hurling's golden era. Many in the club thought I was the second-coming. Another Kiltormer man Tony Frehill had joined them in the early eighties and was a vital cog in their first two county titles in 1984 and 1987. But unfortunately for all concerned, the only similarity between us was the route we took.

It never happened there for me and although I registered the club's first score in 1989 senior championship, by 1992, I was based in Dublin and my star at the club had plummeted.

Demoted to the second team, I was substituted in the 1992 junior hurling final at half time, dejected but understanding why. That was to be the last time I played.

By then I had met my Joan in 1991 and we were married in four years.

In all my years in Dublin, I never got involved in a GAA club.

Now I'm not an eejit but I behaved like one. Looking back it just didn't dawn on me to join a club.

And I am sure if someone had put me on the spot about playing or participating, I'd certainly have considered it.

Joan grew up in Rolestown and it was only natural that we would return to live there in 2003 with our son Michael.

It was by chance that Michael was in the same class as Daniel Sammon whose father David was mentor with the Fingal Raven's U-9 football team.

By pure coincidence I met Dave on a plane going to Frankfurt in January 2008.

He had heard Mikey was pretty good at football and enquired if Mikey would like to play with Ravens. Mikey as it happened had no real interest in it although he remained active in sport.

Now that might have been the end of the conversation had I not heard Dave was involved in a new juvenile hurling set up in the neighbouring village of Oldtown. I took the opportunity to quiz him about it and that's when things started to fall into place.

He filled me in and we exchanged numbers. Immediately a multitude of scenarios began entering in my head. I had figured by then that if I joined an established hurling team, I was unlikely to get a game... too old and way past it!

They'd say it's a "mid-life crisis", I had taken a mere 5,696 days off before attempting a "comeback" ... and it's not as if anyone had missed me. Also what GAA team would entertain the likes of me to come out of a retirement to warm up a bench? At the level I would be playing at, there wouldn't even be any benches!

While hurling was a game I had a passion for as a player and as a spectator, people would think I was crazy to come out of retirement at my age.

I decided to piggyback on the new juvenile hurling set up, try to establish an adult team and give them the benefit of an adult outlet? One can't survive long-term without the other.

I hadn't heard from Dave for a few weeks until I bumped into him again at a local national school charity event in Kettles.

I got his opinion on starting up a team from scratch. He, like Joan, thought the idea had merit, so it was a relief to know I was not entirely mad.

We talked at the bar and after a few minutes Dave motioned over 'Flats'. Sean 'Flats' Flatley was from Castlegar, once a village on the outskirts of Galway. Now it's at the end of the M4, well and truly in the city. Back then Castlegar were a big noise, the first Galway club to win the All-Ireland Club, in a team backboned by seven Connollys. So it was only natural that Sean played the game.

'Flats' and I had once shared the same field in Loughrea in 1989. The occasion was the Ryan Cup final with Garbally up against Moneenageisha Vocational school.

They had just won the All-Ireland which gave us an extra incentive to get one over on our neighbours.

I played corner-forward in a team that also included Cathal Moran and Brendan Keogh who would go on to play with Galway and win three All-Ireland club titles with Athenry in the nineties.

We won well that day but I didn't get to see anything of Sean who at corner-back was on the opposing wing to me.

Like myself, Sean had also lost touch with his club back home after moving to the capital, where he married a local girl from Saint Margaret's in North county Dublin.

His busy schedule with SR Technics in Dublin Airport where he was a mechanic meant that hurling was temporarily parked before he eventually got involved as mentor with the new juvenile hurling set up in The Wild Geese after being approached by Dave.

So now after almost 19 years, myself and Sean would again find ourselves in each other's company albeit in closer proximity and on the same side.

Both of us had our heads down that day in Loughrea but much like Oldtown revolutionary Mollie Weston, I had answered a call to arms.

However my childhood days were filled watching American westerns and I had taken on the role of Yul Brynner in 'The Magnificent Seven'.

Now I needed a few more gunslingers than that and not necessarily of that calibre. I didn't know if Oldtown was ready for us but I was willing to take that chance and so I asked Sean delicately.

'Would you play?'

'Jesus are you mad?' he replied but I had seen too much of my life pass by to take no for an answer and eventually he agreed to join up as goalkeeper and mentor.

Also in the gathering that night was Peter Dunphy, a second cousin of Henry Shefflin but curiously enough not our only connection with the Kilkenny team as you will find out later. Peter liked what he heard and was on board immediately. A garda, he lives 400 metres from me in Rolestown but I did not know him. Peter is hurling 24/7 and originally hails from Mooncoin in Kilkenny

He had played with them before doing tours of hurling duty with Garda and St.Finians, Swords where he played at a fairly decent level.

He had not played since 1995 but I found his knowledge of the game was immense.

Always well informed on the hurling scene from inter-county to juvenile level, he like Sean Flatley had a strong grounding which would sustain us well over the forthcoming campaigns.

So by the end of the evening, there was quite a bounce in my step and I remember saying to Dave Sammon later, half serious/half joking, that we had a 'fifth of a team after just one night'.

Dave himself said he could not play but his encouragement and assistance at this early stage was invaluable.

CHAPTER 3
RECRUITMENT COMMENCES

The four of us reconvened the following Tuesday in the empty lounge of the local pub, Oldtown House. It was agreed then that the Wild Geese GAA club, where the juvenile hurling had started the previous year, was the ideal base for the formation of a new adult hurling team.

Previously Oldtown had formed part of a bigger parish along with Garristown, Ballymadun and Rolestown.

It was subsequently paired alongside Rolestown and as a result the local school was badly attended for the best part of 10 to 15 years prior to an influx at the start of the new millennium.

In the interim period, the club was seriously hampered by its lack of numbers and was never able to get a juvenile football section off the ground.

This meant that many of the villages' brightest young talents had to go elsewhere for their football and while there were hopes they would return at some stage, that never materialised in a lot of cases.

In particular there has been serious bitterness between the likes of Wild Geese and Rolestown club Fingal Ravens over the years.

If you look at that Ravens team that won the Dublin intermediate championship in 2006, there were at least four or five of them that were born, bred and reared in Oldtown

Now, if they had returned to play for the Wild Geese, they would probably be in Junior 'A' and not Junior D, where they are today.

That's a lot of ifs and buts there but that's the hard cold reality of it. As it was the Geese were consigned to play in the lower scale of the leagues and championships while at the time their neighbours Garristown, St.Margaret's, Ballyboughal and Ravens were competing at Junior A or higher with Ravens at the time of writing having two teams operating in the top four Adult divisions.

So in that area, the Wild Geese were the least successful having only had one football team that folded twice in the previous six years.

This, Dublin smallest club could not be deemed a threat to its Gaelic football-only neighbours, were we would be doing some of our hurling recruiting.

The four clubs mentioned above were Gaelic Football only Clubs and did not offer hurling and even if Dublin had a parish rule like most of the other counties in Ireland, any hurlers from these clubs could then come to us.

All this Gaelic Football carry-on was a benefit to us in many ways, making the Wild Geese the ideal launch club for hurling. In addition the recruiters were all 'blow ins' with no previous history and completely neutral and oblivious to any bad history between the clubs in the locality.

And with the backing of the Wild Geese club chairman, Sean McNulty, who saw the potential, the recruitment drive was put into action the following weekend.

The plan was to get round the dressing-rooms and visit the neighbouring clubs and talk to the players.

We hadn't made a formal approach to any of the GAA clubs as we were not sure how the hierarchy of these GFCs would look at it. Already they had many of their juveniles coming to Oldtown to play hurling since 2007 but targeting adult players was a different issue, given the pressures that could come with playing and training in both codes.

We felt that if we could get a few players from every club that word of mouth would be the biggest conveyor belt for us.

Together with this, flyers were put on the vehicles outside the regions' churches during mass times. 'Looking for adults to form a hurling team' and 'no previous experience required' they read. Dave and I did the car parks of the seven church car parks in our catchment area.

As it happened Collie Prenderville, who I had watched a year earlier in Croke Park when Fingal Ravens played Moycullen in the All

Ireland intermediate football championship final, came out from mass to find the flyer on his car – that's how he heard about it.

Collie, an Oldtown native whose brother plays with the Wild Geese football team, was one of 'those' who had elected to stay with the Ravens after a promising juvenile career with them and I am told that decision caused some controversy at the time.

But he had always wanted to give hurling a go and having never played with his village team, you could say we had become the answer to his prayers.

We also posted the flyers through the letter boxes of the housing estates in the region and hammered them onto the various notice boards.

By now the local paper 'The Fingal Independent' was also running with the story in the sports pages about what we were trying to do, while I visited the local dressing-rooms after Gaelic football training.

The reception I got was amazing even if there were many jokes along the lines of 'who would give those mad men sticks'.

Nonetheless, the idea proved appealing as it became the subject of some discussion in the local dressing-rooms. Football was very much king in North County Dublin, so we were unsure what the reaction would be.

For example, the day I went up to the Wild Geese football training and spoke to the lads openly about our plans and hopes, the reaction I got was fantastic and that was largely down to John Rennie.

He was the first to embrace it followed by most of the others present. He was definitely the most enthusiastic of our new converts and he even took it upon himself to inform those not present by text.

From the moment I met him that evening, I was convinced he believed in the whole concept.

He was also to prove a very effective recruiter in the early stages and did his best to ensure that most if not all of his friends signed up for the cause.

That's how Ciaran Smith heard about it. Indeed after that evening we had seven or eight new converts – at least for a while.

The numbers that committed were high at an early stage so we were confident we would have enough bodies for a team. The football mentors did not seem to mind but in fairness most of the lads made their own decisions on this.

And for now quantity was the main issue; quality was parked, to be dealt with at a much later date.

Things moved very quickly after that. Patsy Hough, a friend and former teammate who I had played in the blue of Kiltormer, was now playing with Castleknock.

He told me there was a spare place in the Junior E Championship and Adult Hurling League Division 7 (AHL7), the latter could be a tall order, as it was not the lowest division – still I was thrilled. As it was April, we thought we may have missed the chance to participate in the 2008 competitions as we were now a few months into the new season.

Sean McNulty however managed to secure these berths for us and to his credit persuaded the Dublin County Board to waive any affiliation fees for our first season.

'Flats' had filled me in on one of the new mentors with the juvenile teams, that he felt may be enticed to play or possibly help out. One evening after juvenile training, I lingered as they finished up, waiting to pounce. I knew Ed Sweetman straight away, even though I had never met him. The brief description I had been given about him was 100 per cent accurate. He was tall, standing at 6'2", dark, lean and took giant strides. I stood in front of him and looked up, introduced myself, briefed him on our plans and asked 'would you like to play?' He stared at me without expression but then gently nodded in agreement without hesitation. 'That was easy' – I thought, pinching myself.

Staring people down was not something new to Ed and he always gave as good as he got no matter what the situation.

Despite his formidable stature, Ed was not exempt from friendly banter from his teammates.

Born and raised in East Wall, Ed was the last of eight children. Before Ed's arrival there were four boys and three girls and I recall him telling me how 'the girls where gutted, when I was born as another girl would have evened out the score'. They did not see much of him in his earlier years with his mother dying when he was just a year old. That's when he moved from Cabra to East Wall to be reared by his aunt and uncle. While his father Lar and his brothers played both codes for St. Finbars, Ed joined up with O'Tooles.

The 'Larriers' as they where more known took their players mainly from East Wall and Ballybough areas and the old clubhouse on Seville Strand had been at centre of the Luftwaffe bombings of 1941 where 28 people lost their lives.

While Fingal is officially part of Dublin, Ed was nonetheless considered a 'blow-in'.

But Ed who still likes to wear his O'Tooles jersey on occasions, was fond of reminding them that his grandfather had moved to Dublin from Ballyboughal at the turn of the last century.

In fact Ed can trace his family roots to Ballyboughal and Westpalstown (town land in Oldtown) to 1720. His great, great grandparents are buried less then one mile from the Wild Geese pitch. He has offered tours of the graveyard to prove it but these have never been taken up!

Ed had spent a bit of time away in the UK during the nineties before coming home with his family, as there was no opportunity to play at a lower level at O'Tooles he hung up the hurl.

So when he came back he 'pitched his tent' in Garristown, a frontier village, four miles due west of Oldtown and nestled along the Dublin-Meath border.

There he would coach football extensively with the local club but hurling was never far from his heart. And to have his experience at that early stage was to prove a big plus for us.

Having being initially wary about the idea of a team in the first place, 'Flats' now was anxious to have the first training session. I was cautious though as I wanted to ensure we had enough expressions of interest before finalising a fixed date. Rather reluctantly I gave in and we fixed for the second Monday in April at 7pm.

RECRUITMENT COMMENCES

The designated night had to be a Monday, as Tuesday and Thursday were nights for football training in the region and it would have been crazy to clash with them. Wednesday was juvenile hurling night. Momentum was building.

CHAPTER 4

THE SULTANS OF SWING

The drive to the grounds is exactly a 10-minute one from my house in Rolestown but it was to prove a long one on that first evening.

While I was reasonably confident that we would get the numbers, no one really knew each other. I felt it was important from the start to be decisive and to give the impression that we were all singing from the same hymn sheet.

Yes my initial impressions of Sean, Peter and Ed were good but talk of their organising and training ability was just that at that stage – talk.

So as I entered the grounds I was a bit anxious knowing if we did not get things right immediately, any impetus we had built up would be lost.

Thankfully though it was not too long before the others were there. Sean had arrived before me with Peter and Ed pulling in shortly after.

And as we waited for the new recruits to arrive I surveyed the scene around me.

The pitch at St Mary's sports grounds in Oldtown, runs east to west, and is tight and bumpy. When tightly cut the grass is just perfect for ground hurling or jab lifts on the run. The car park is situated at the eastern end as you drive in straight ahead is an indoor handball alley which is owned by the Oldtown racquetball and handball club.

It's the first fortified hurling handball alley of its kind in Ireland and was built a good 45 years ago.

Inside is a maple floor which is '40x20' and there is a balcony review area but that has gone downhill.

Indeed in intervening years down there I think I have only seen it being used once. Originally it was part of Wild Geese but the handball racquetball crowd went their own way.

Beside that are two dressing rooms which are both quite plain, the 1970s architectural style is evident but hey, they are more than sufficient. The early sessions were tricky in terms of the high numbers that attended.

In the first year alone I'd say we saw about 60 players and it didn't start to level out until the third season.

There were lots of questions from us like; 'Have you played hurling before?' and 'what position?'

Getting a measure of their character was another thing but many of those we came across that first night would become regular fixtures at the grounds over the following seasons.

John Rennie was the first to pull up at the grounds that evening. He arrived with his younger brother Dave and Peter McGowan.

Almost immediately I was struck by his height as he was sitting the first time I met him. We would find out he was not shy in using it to his advantage on the field.

At 6'5 (Dave came in at 6'2) and a senior fund accountant with HSBC, he certainly had an aura about him.

At an early stage Sean and I had decided he would be the right candidate for captain. Admittedly we never really considered anyone else. From what we had seen he had a bubbly personality and got on with everyone.

We had figured he would bring those leadership qualities to the field but as a former hurler with Fingallians, John probably had set the bar too high in terms of expectations of his teammates.

You have to remember this was our maiden season but it wasn't too long before he was chastising teammates for not giving an accurate pass.

Opponents would also get a few tasty words thrown their way while referees would sometimes get the full treatment.

Often he would stand there with his arms spread wide towering over them and asking why they had given a free against us.

This was to earn him the nickname 'The statue of Rennie' from his team-mates.

We were 'a glass half full' sort of team and these antics were not helpful at this early stage in the team's progress.

These small faults aside, his contributions were what we looked for in a forward. While his stature meant that he was never going to be light on his feet, he nonetheless ticked the boxes in terms of being a target man.

A very effective poacher, he was always worth a few scores to us and at this level if all our forwards had come back with the same return, I reckon we'd have won a lot more games.

Like Ed, Shane Byrne who happened to be my brother-in-law also had his hurling roots in the inner city where he was an accomplished player at the local secondary school, James Street Christian brothers, while also 'guesting' occasionally for the Liffey Gaels Junior 'A' Team in later years.

He had not committed to any club and almost slipped from our grasp. Twenty years old, standing at 5'8, built like an Ox with a 'Jarhead' hair cut, he was a trainee carpenter. I didn't really know much about him except that he played soccer. I put that ignorance on my behalf down to the substantial age gap between us.

But while he was at a family dinner one night at my home he spotted my new hurling helmet at the bottom of the stairs and asked about it.

Joan filled him in on the developments and we were both amazed to hear that hurling was his first love in sport and that he'd be delighted to be part of the new team. I was as much relieved to have discovered this then as to have missed such low-hanging fruit would have been a big embarrassment.

To have a family member with the right age profile and of decent hurling ability join us at this early stage was of huge benefit and very encouraging.

There may have been a perception that because he was part of my extended family he might receive preferential treatment.

If anything it was the reverse, there would be no hiding place for him and as it transpired, we had the occasional run-in.

Shane however was competitive and ambitious and from the start became a vital part of the jigsaw.

Philly McCarthy was another from the six plus category and his entrance proved something of a grand one.

I was at that stage busy taking the details of the various players before hurrying them along to the dressing-rooms and then out to the others.

I took a brief respite from the proceedings to talk with one of the new arrivals, Tom Smyth.

Tom as it transpired was the grandson of Tommy Butler, a member of the Fingal Rovers team who were an adult hurling team that played for a few seasons in the 1950s. So we now had a good blood connection with that team.

As we stood chatting, we were distracted by a sound of a Red Ford Focus ST 2.2 sports car roaring around the corner and up the hill into the car park.

Dust was flying and the music was blaring and suitably distracted I asked Tom 'Do you know who your man is?'

Tom, a master farrier, replied: 'That's Philly McCarthy, he plays football with St Colmcilles in Swords.'

I asked: 'How come he is coming out here to play, sure Fingallians is across the road from Colmcilles

Tom replied: 'True, but those clubs hate each other – he couldn't play with the enemy!'

'Jesus we'll have a team of giants at this rate' I added as I saw him step out of the car. Although McCarthy is a great Irish name, we found out he was one-quarter German and one-quarter Scottish.

Not exactly hurling heartlands but we needn't have worried – Philly knew what to do with the hurl.

His first preference has always been football and he hadn't played hurling since his primary school days in Marino.

Surprisingly for such a big lad, he proved very mobile.

He could drive points from midfield and his ball-winning skills in the middle third certainly made him a formidable opponent.

And while Philly liked to keep moving, he could slot into almost any position although midfield or wing back was his preferred choice.

He even did a slot at full-back for a while although he found it a bit boring there.

It was just a matter of what he could do for the team on the day. And Philly was always someone who made himself available.

Even this season he changed two shifts to be there for the lads, even though he was injured. So both on and off the pitch he proved a huge influence and from an early stage was certainly a good addition to the team.

After the first two to three training sessions we had a fair idea about our strengths. One of the biggest challenges for Ed and the rest of the selectors was the diversity of talents and personalities.

As Ed said: 'In O'Tooles you grew up with lads and they didn't need to be told what to do.'

Everyone already knew each other strengths and weaknesses, but here we all had to figure each other out.

It was a case of expecting more from certain lads than others while always remembering that we were playing at a fairly low level of junior hurling'.

Our work ethic was important and from early on we saw that the more effort we put into it, the more we were getting out of it.

Sometimes when things weren't going well, it was a case of just persevering. Some lads hadn't a clue how to hurl and after a few sessions, they gave up. We were lucky that even if those who stayed beyond the initial burst never played competitively before they had mostly held a hurl at some time or other in the past.

Two players in particular who are still with us, Ciaran Smith and Nathan McCaffrey, were in the 'never held a hurl before' category. From the start, however, both applied themselves extremely well.

Ciaran was 30 when he started playing and Nathan was the youngest at 16. We were to play him in our first game but in theory we shouldn't have, as the minimum age is 16.

But he was very eager and dedicated and his father also wanted him to play. Nathan proved to be a quick learner.

When he began, he had this huge big swing and was getting

blocked down all the time. He perfected his swing as time went on and now there is no better man on the team to block an opponent as well.

He has shortened his grip and now he plays off left and right.

Nathan's pace was another big plus. He's like Usain Bolt with a hurl but at that stage he was still developing his game. He was so fast he could outrun his opponent but because he wasn't confident with his swing, some times then he would resort to kicking the sliotar.

We warned him many times: 'Nathan keep doing that and you'll lose a foot.' We there afraid with his foot being so close to the sliotar, it would get hit though I admit an opponent would still have had to catch him first.

Thankfully now he is hitting balls on the run. Overall I think he has the potential to be a superb hurler especially when he fills out a bit.

At the other end of the scale, Ciaran was the eldest of that batch that had never played before. Nonetheless he was an impressive character. A native of Swords, Ciaran was a former corporal in the Irish army with a Lebanon tour of duty under his belt.

A fully trained medic who now serves as winchman with the Irish Coast guard helicopter based at Dublin Airport. A great man with a penchant for triathlons.

Like Peter Dunphy, Ciaran also had Kilkenny connections with his mother a distant relation of Adrian Ronan.

Ciaran was another to have received John Rennie's 'call to arms' text and while enthusiastic about the project, he wasn't convinced it would be a success. Despite his lack of expertise he worked hard at his game.

This was not always easy for guys like Ciaran due to work commitments. When he was not always able to train he made up for it by practising at home. Just this season he purchased the 'pucca' which is like a hurling swing ball. You hit it back and forth. The club has got two of them on the go.

It is something that helps and for guys that might not be able train due to work commitments and haven't access to a wall, it certainly keeps their touch up.

And in Ciaran's case, the work has paid off.

One thing that he had in buckets was fearlessness and it certainly served the club well a couple of years ago.

GAA grounds have in the past been targeted by would-be thieves where players perhaps unwisely leave their possessions in cars during training and match days.

There was an incident at our grounds a while back during football training. Two dodgy-looking lads pulled into the car park to watch what was going on. The then football trainer Pat Brown challenged them whereby one of them produced an iron-bar and the other a combat knife. By a twist of fate, Ciaran Smith had arrived late and immediately spotted what was going on. He advised the two gurriers that he was about to retrieve his hurl from the car, upon which they hopped back into their car and sped off.

CHAPTER 5

FOR THOSE WHO ARE ABOUT TO TRY, WE SALUTE YOU

The most pleasing thing for me about the initial turnouts was the mixed representations from many Gaelic football only clubs; we were becoming a raggle-taggle conglomerate. The first St. Margarets GFC representative was Sean Madigan. Sean was a hugely popular and well-known figure and would go on to be our team captain in 2009.

He is the son of Mary Madigan who had done sterling work at administrative level with St Margarets.

Given that she had played camogie with Meath and could claim Joachim Kelly as a blood relative, it was perhaps only fitting that Sean had also gravitated towards the small ball game.

He was immediately sold on the whole idea. For him it was Fingal all rolled into one and no matter what parish you were from, it was still Fingal.

Sean was just blown away by the dressing-room atmosphere. It was something he had never experienced playing with any other team and to him it was absolutely phenomenal how all of north county Fingal came together under one group.

In truth, he came with a bit of pedigree having started hurling with St. Sylvesters while also receiving his secondary school education at Colaiste Choilm Swords.

This school was well known for its GAA prowess and three pupils from the one class alone would go on to manage AFL teams in the one season.

Joe Kettle took charge of Ballyboughal that won promotion to Division 3 in 2010 while Adrian Henchy with the St Pat's Donabate club joined him a season later.

Alan Hanrahan completed that trio when he took charge of

Fingallians but while football was strong at Colaiste Choilm, there was also a good hurling connection too.

The leading lights there during Sean's time were Theo Farrell and Brother Maher from Tipperary.

You had a lot of the christian brothers there as well and according to Sean some of them would have had a bigger interest in football and hurling than they did in education so in a way hurling was a good way out of class work at times.

As Sean put it: 'You went out and trained but you had to put the effort in training.'

After finishing with St Sylvester's and the brothers, Sean took a break from hurling for many moons but was still actively involved with the football in Margaret's.

Sean is very like a lot of us; he may lack a bit of pace but he never lost his love for hurling.

And from the start he was on board with the project and even suggested we should change our name to 'Wild Fingal.'

I did not give it much thought at the time as things were snowballing but in hindsight the different name had merit and might have allowed us to cast our net even further.

I thought Wild Geese was a great name and in fact our adopted club is the only GAA Club which uses it in Ireland.

That said it's fair to say many do not understand its meaning. One of the Fingal Ravens lads wondered one day why the North County Dublin clubs were fascinated with birds' names for their clubs.

I gave him a brief history lesson and hope he picked up its importance.

The term Wild Geese referred to Irish soldiers who left to serve as mercenaries in continental European armies in the 16th, 17th and 18th centuries.

As amateurs who give up their time to play for a unified cause you could never refer to our players as 'mercenaries' but there was, nonetheless, that sense of adventure for those arriving into Oldtown and going into battle for the first time.

One of those was Mark Kealy from the Starlights club on Collinstown lane, a popular spot for plane spotters as it is located beside the airport.

Mark's landing among us was a quiet one. He had heard about us from a friend of a father and when he discovered that evening that we already had a goalkeeper, his comment was; 'looks like I will have to do some running.'

Straight away, like Sean Madigan, he saw there was a 'good buzz' and enjoyed the fact there were lads from different clubs.

The wide diversity leads immediately to a healthy curiosity and respect between teammates. This camaraderie would gel the team together for the future.

It's the attention to detail, however irrelevant it might seem, that can prove the difference in the end.

For Ed it was socks. Ed combined coaching with playing in those early days and one of his earlier instructions was to bring the right coloured socks which were black in this case.

For Ed it was all about winning battles. And that was the thing with O'Tooles. 'They were always great for winning battles,' he would say time and again.

Some of the boys used to slag him because he only knew one way to train. But if the ball was there he felt you had to go for it.

Hence the need to bring the right pair of socks.

The logic of that was that if they were playing matches or training matches and they had black coloured socks on (which is part of the Wild Geese strip) he wouldn't pull on them while trying to get possession of the sliotar.

If they hadn't got the right ones and he happened to pull on a player from his own team, it would be likely be their own fault as Mattie Lambe – who would go on to be our most decorated player -would soon discover.

Now Mattie had picked up more injuries from playing football with Ravens then he ever did playing hurling, thereby debunking the myth that hurling is a more dangerous game.

It transpired that two of the worst belts he got from playing were from Ed in training. And he still has the scars to prove it – one on his right knee and the other on the left shin.

Ed's single-mindedness and focus certainly held us in good stead in those first sessions.

Himself and Peter had it well sussed with a wide variety of drills which were designed to assess the levels of hurling competence. And with the amount of kicking of sliotars that went on initially, we knew we were challenged to improve our stick work.

Ed asked each player where they played, then watched to see if they were comfortable there. His strategy was to place most of the big, strong lads at the back and put the fit lads in the middle.

Perhaps understandably Ed reckoned 'everyone wanted to be a forward'. It was a strategy from the start to give the team a good backbone and it worked because defensively we were a mean team.

The lack of natural forwards was to be our Achilles heel as is the case with most hurling teams regardless of the level.

Anyway the 'new' recruits were divided into groups of three. Ground hurling and then lift and strike without handling the ball or running with it. After that there was lifting, carrying and striking and to finish off a 20 minute game of backs and forwards. In all cases, whether a player hit off their left or right, dexterous hurlers was what we were aiming for, even from the beginning. At any level of hurling it can be easy to read a player's intentions if he only has one side. We preached this a lot.

In total, 16 turned up that first evening and as Ed walked off the field he commented 'some lads looked like Christy Ring when they were pucking around and doing the drills but when they were marked by another player the truth soon came out'.

During coaching talks he tended to reference Christy Ring and I recall overhearing two of the budding hurlers whispering to one another; 'who is this Christy Ring Ed is always on about?' The other replied: 'I think he played for O'Tooles with Ed'.

From the mouths of babes!

Anyway by week three, the numbers at training had grown to 24, as word began to spread.

Nonetheless Ed felt that 'some of the most enthusiastic were not great hurlers while some classy hurlers did not have the grit to be great.' Shane Byrne had both in equal amounts even at that early stage. The best thing about the squad was that there was a place for every one in the great scheme.

CHAPTER 6
ONE SUMMER'S EVE

It was the middle of May when we got notice from the Dublin GAA County Board of our first fixture.

Sean McNulty had come in with a piece of paper in his hand. Straight away we were thrown in at the deep end with a first round tie in the Junior E Championship away to Setanta on Friday May 23rd at 7.30 pm.

There was consternation mixed with sheer excitement in the dressing-room when we announced our date with destiny.

'But we haven't even played a challenge' said 'Flanno'. Martin 'Flanno' Flanagan was one part of a strong Fingal Raven's contingent that was with us from the start.

Collie Prenderville and Richard 'Dickser' Daly followed 'Flanno' soon after and all three adapted to the hurling fairly quickly.

The Ravens connection was important and the likes of Ravens manager Mick Deegan were very supportive. We had three or four players on the Ravens team and they were going very well at the time in the senior championship for the time ever in their history in 2008.

And he was fair about it. Those lads were playing senior one football at a top level while we were at the lowest level in hurling. He could have easily said you are not playing hurling.

But they took the hurling seriously. And he was right about a challenge but it had never entered my mind to arrange a game. I just figured that when we had the numbers and had sharpened up a bit, we would just dive straight in.

By this stage the numbers at the weekly training session had settled a bit and we had a fair idea of our starting 15. How they would perform was another thing.

In any case we had been doing well at the training and while it did prove difficult for some of the older lads I felt we were ready for lift off.

However there were some things you just couldn't account for and a few weeks before our maiden game, we met with an unlikely hitch when 'Flats' damaged his wrist.

He had been out cycling with his daughter Ciara, when she inadvertently swerved across the road in front of him. Sean went straight over the crossbar, suffering severe ligament damage.

His wrist was in a cast and he was out of work for a few weeks but was still determined to make his hurling comeback regardless of his minor handicap.

Playing in a specialist position, he was someone we couldn't afford to be without. As our designated goalkeeper, Sean was an excellent shot-stopper who could also get amazing distances on his puck outs.

He would consistently drop the sliotar onto the opposing 45m line. In the summer with the hard ground they could arrive at the 20m line. Our puck-out tactics were simple – just pick a side.

If it worked, stick with it, if not rotate it to the other side or just straight down the middle. I was dead against short puck-outs. If you can gain ground, take it. And Sean's big puck-outs were a big plus for an inexperienced team like us.

Hurling ability aside, he was also a straight shooter. When he texted me a few hours before the game complaining of butterflies that worried me a bit. What tormented him most was 'the big feckin' bandage' he still sported from his injury.

Our first match was played on a warm sunny summer's evening with the skies overhead clear and only a light westerly breeze to worry about.

My son Michael was receiving his First Communion on the following day which meant that my parents had travelled up.

My father PJ had accompanied me to the pitch but the last memory of the day was the parting shot from Joan which was 'to avoid injury'.

The game was on Setanta's second pitch, a Fingal County Council owned field in Popintree, Ballymun. It was strange walking it with my dad after all this time.

My love affair with the game began when my father and his young family parachuted into Kiltormer in East Galway in 1980.

Our arrival came at a time when Kiltormer were enjoying unbridled success in the county and my memories of that time were joyful ones.

A crowd of 12,000 attended the 1982 senior decider, played in August, when they overcame bitter rivals Castlegar by a two-point margin and PJ, the local Garda Sergeant, was already faced with a decision.

He was a pioneer and had seen the perils of alcohol on many occasions. But he decided to cut the locals some slack with the 11 pm closing time stretched. The three pubs in the village were swinging for days as celebrations surpassed anything that ever went before.

I caught the hurling bug after that and my father was always there to attend my matches. He would have been very honest in his appraisal. If I was bad he would tell me I was bad and more often than not I was bad.

In some ways it drove me on but in hindsight I believe you are better off to go with the positive where you think your glass is half full.

That said I was glad to have him by my side for my comeback as we walked onto the pitch. He had never played competitive hurling, only football. He encouraged me to play and often played with me and enthused about the game by saying: 'it's in us all'. In a remarkable career, he played senior football in five counties, played in three senior finals in three different counties but unfortunately lost them all. His father before him had played in six county senior finals, winning three but when he retired he lost all interest in the game. He only saw my father play twice. PJ did not make the same mistake with his children but I'm sure he had figured his days of going to my games were over.

This was a setting far removed from the bustling Kiltormer of my youth. In the background you could see the towers of flats which were then synonymous with the Ballymun landscape.

There we encountered a lone man putting up the nets. A big, tall ginger-haired chap with a strong country accent, Gearoid McGrath from south Tipperary, was born to lead and instruct. Captain of the team, he was also a renowned adult referee as we were to discover later on in the season.

Anyway having confirmed to us that we were at the right venue, we began to tog out under the trees.

By now, a decent crowd had assembled. Many had travelled from Oldtown and Rolestown to witness our first game. Most were worried-looking wives and girlfriends as well as some curious onlookers who no doubt were wondering what to make of these' 'mad men with sticks'. (And in the case of one player their fears certainly came to fruition).

Decked out in the yellow jerseys kindly donated by the Wild Geese footballers, we started our warm-up routine during which time some complained about the firmness of the ground, others the length of the grass.

In fairness it was below par for a hurling game but there was nothing we could do. Soon it was time for the throw in but it was then I realised there was no referee. I went over to Gearóid and to his credit he was already on the case. He got no joy from the appointed referee but after making a few calls eventually got one positive response. While we were waiting, the faces on Paddy Jones and Chris Keane said 'nerves' but all the while this was happening the minutes for me seemed to pass like hours. I thought initially that we might have to postpone the game which would have been a major anti-climax. Forty five minutes later, the man in black took to the field.

He blew the whistle with authority to announce his arrival. John Rennie went forward for the toss. I could hear the Setanta captain ask him 'who are yous? Googled ya and only came up with mercenaries.'

He was referring to the film 'The Wild Geese' who had been sent in to overthrow a vicious dictator in central Africa.

John smirked and gave him the edited version while at the same time losing the toss.

Our maiden game had finally started. While no church bells were ringing, this was a momentous and truly remarkable occasion for us.

The game was hardly five minutes old when we had our first interruption. The Setanta wing-forward had brought his hurl down sharply on Shane's helmet.

Some of our lads struggled to keep Shane who was playing at centre back from rattling the offender in retaliation. Unsurprisingly the culprit did not take to being told off by the referee and the ensuing argument only got worse when Gearoid tried to intervene. Oblivious to the calming calls from his captain, the culprit ripped off his helmet, flung it to the ground with his hurl before storming off while shouting at us. He paraded off the pitch, off the park and duly out of sight. What a turbulent start to our hurling Odyssey!'

After the dust had settled, Setanta were the first to get on top with a series of scores.

A great point from Collie Prenderville settled our nerves and it was perhaps appropriate that the honour of the recording the first ever Wild Geese score was bestowed on an Oldtown native.

That opening point will undoubtedly have allowed him to exorcise a few ghosts but more importantly it had a re-assuring effect on us with John then drawing us level with two pointed frees.

Setanta surprisingly made two early substitutions but it had an instant effect as they tacked on two points from play.

They added a goal soon after albeit a rather fortuitous one. The sliotar had become embedded in the middle of a busy goalmouth as both sets of players attempted to make contact with the mercurial object.

Time seemed to stand still before one of the Setanta forwards scooped the pass past our goal line, which meant by half-time we trailed by 1-5 to 0-4.

As we huddled together, initially the discussion was jovial as a sort of giddy childishness descended as we recalled how their lad had walked off. Peter and Ed eventually settled everyone down, highlighting that this was a game we could win and while we were four points adrift, the general consensus was that we were doing okay.

Good advice was given and one change was made with Nathan who was just two months shy of his 16th birthday coming into the full forward line.

Nathan took the game very seriously and as the fastest man on the panel certainly gave us an extra dimension on the turnover.

The second-half saw us open our account courtesy of a long range free from David Rennie to leave us just a goal behind. But we continued to trail our hosts despite scores from Dick Daly and John Rennie.

With three minutes to go, Setanta still held a goal advantage over us. But taking a leaf out of Packie Bonner's notebook when the Irish goalkeeper delivered a massive kick-out to set up Niall Quinn for the equaliser against Holland at Italia 90, 'Flats' stepped up to the plate to set up our all important score.

His huge puck-out found 'Flanno' on the forty who cleverly doubled on the ball as the Setanta full-back line pushed out.

This left Nathan free and as he slipped past the stunned backs, leaned down with just one hand on the hurl to gather up the sliotar.

Now only 20 metres separated him and their goal. The Setanta goalkeeper ventured out menacingly in an attempt to impede him.

But with the delicacy of a man lighting a fuse, he discreetly tapped it passed the keeper and the sliotar strolled across the line. As a precaution our other corner-forward Danny Kelly followed up to make sure of the score.

David Sammon was our umpire and he had the pleasure of raising the green flag and there followed huge celebrations on the line with Nathan's family watching proudly on.

When the final whistle blew I actually thought we had lost by a point while the lads on the line thought we had won. It was neither with the referee confirming that the game ended in a draw, 1-9 each.

There was a lot of back slapping and satisfaction amongst our group and personally I was thrilled with the outcome. While I realised that we had not become a panel of bona fide hurlers overnight, we had pushed many of these rookies to run before they could toddle or walk and this was a meaningful result.

Any scepticism about our ability to master the basic skills of hurling as a unit was parked for now. This was an achievement, with eight North County Dublin Gaelic football clubs represented on the field that evening. The Wild Geese revolution had begun and the air of optimism was there for all to breathe.

CHAPTER 7
LEAP IN THE DARK

Like Ballymun, Dolphins Barn is another disadvantaged area but nonetheless itself and Crumlin beside it are two villages with a good GAA tradition.

Kevin's played their hurling in Dolphin Park which had also been home to St Francis FC, a non-league soccer team who under Peter Mahon made it to the FAI Cup final in 1990.

Kevin's was one of only three hurling clubs in Dublin

and as fate would have it we drew these two straight into our inaugural season.

They were to be our next opponents and coming three days after the championship bow against Setanta, it was perhaps understandable that our lads took to the field still brimming with confidence three days later.

But as the only league slot our chairman could secure for us was Division 7, the second lowest in the adult hurling league, we were expecting a tough encounter.

And Kevin's certainly played with a slickness and style we had not witnessed before but with our physicality we felt we were prepared for most eventualities.

Initially we had some degree of success against Kevin's forward line which we managed to close down as they got closer to goal. Nonetheless they managed to counteract that by popping over scores from further out. By half-time the writing was on the wall and I was already asking myself what had we let ourselves in for.

Most of the lads had played football over the weekend and were noticeably tired. Then in the corner of my eye, I spotted Sean Madigan in an apparent scrap with his helmet. 'Are you alright there, Sean?' I asked.

'I can't see out through the bloody helmet guard' he replied.

His wife Barbara had just had a baby, their fourth, so we had not seen much of him since the opening sessions. Needless to say the helmet and his head had not been afforded the necessary bonding time. There were no hacksaws in the first aid kit but he found a scissors that assisted him in taking off the guard.

It was a small victory though as we were beaten on a resounding scoreline of 3-17 to 0-6 in the end.

Certainly Kevin's were one of a few teams we played that season who were light years ahead of us and the disappointing thing was that we didn't even get the opportunity to intimidate them. Defensive walls that can be applied in big ball games just do not work in hurling and we could not stem the tide.

But not every setback is a mortal blow and we knew we were on a journey, so the disappointment felt by most of us was minimal. It was a wake-up call and no heads dropped as we accepted we had come up against a superior team.

On an encouraging note three new players approached me about joining up. I figured that if they came this far to see us they must be serious and from that evening Mattie Lambe and his two friends David Green and Tom Draper (grandson of the famous Arkle trainer) were added to the panel.

An added bonus was that all three where from the Oldtown area and while Lambe was a slow burner when it came to hurling he was to make a serious impact in time.

Our first home game was in the championship against St. Joseph's/O'Connell Boys, an amalgamated team from the north inner city who came with a tough reputation.

Ed went to school with a lot of them at St Joseph's CBS in Marino, a famed GAA establishment that was home to a lot of the Vincent's lads that graced the great Dublin football team of the seventies.

New heroes, however, were starting to emerge in the Dublin 3 area. The likes of ·Sean Kearns and John Thompson, the latter a neighbour of Ed's who became a fixture on the Dublin hurling team in the eighties.

While David Beckham would be the poster boy for many a kid

growing up, Ed's proud boast was that he secured Thompson's autograph by the age of 10.

As a juvenile Ed played and trained alongside the seniors, albeit on the adjoining pitch at their old base in St Anne's.

It was an added thrill to be able to watch the older O'Tooles lads when they put on the Dublin shirt. Ed was a dyed-in-the wool hurler but like many of his former classmates, this was new territory.

It certainly added spice to a game which was fixed for Friday 6th June. Needless to say sub-editors at the local newspaper, the Fingal Independent, rather aptly ran 'D-Day for the Wild Geese' hurlers as their headline in their preview for the game.

This local media interest helped create awareness of our existence and build a profile for us with the people of north county Dublin. Word of mouth though was still the biggest recruitment agent we had.

An enthusiastic crowd of curious onlookers turned up on the sunny evening of the game. It was a tight affair which we were always chasing but not that far away.

For a lot of guys new to the game it was a learning curve. Most of them were footballers and you could see that. Too often they moved the ball with their feet instead of their hurl whereas with the juveniles they automatically used their hurls to move it.

Personally I was working hard too to get my touch back (it took two years) but I still knew how to use my head and be physical when over the sliotar.

Whenever I came up against defenders and particularly those with good hurling instinct, I would let them get close to me before I took my shot and then try to push them away.

I felt we gave a good account of ourselves against Josephs that evening with Ed giving an inspirational team talk at the interval.

In those early days our team talks were more about persuasion than giving orders. My son Michael heard the talk that day and innocently said to his mother: 'Ed certainly used the 'F' word a lot!'

Ed's 'persuasiveness' however was not enough that evening with the visitors running out winners on a 2-11 to 1-10 scoreline.

That night was also the first time I came across our '16th man' who although not playing would become a good source of scores for us in the following seasons.

Vincy Fitzpatrick is an elderly gentleman who worked as a farm labourer in the area and cycled everywhere. He did not drive or own a car. Just before most home games commenced, he would pedal into the park and makes his way over to the referee.

It is normally only in high profile occasions that referees come with their own umpires and linesmen. Officials from competing clubs usually man the breach at all other games but reluctantly so. This is because such volunteers are the subject of so much 'abuse' from supporters that they are not inclined to go back too often.

Under such circumstances, referees were delighted (early on) to have Vincy, a very decent man, offer his services. From his own point of view, he gave a new meaning to the term 'moving the goal posts'.

Any 50/50 calls at our goals were always signalled wide, while if we got close to scoring, particularly points, Vincy was inclined to award them. Once or twice it led to confusion and disbelief from the visitors.

Alex Ferguson claimed that having Peter Schmeichel was worth a few extra points before the season started... well we could say the same of Vincy.

We went back to the local pub after the game. Many of the lads or their partners made sandwiches and it was the first time we came across Flats' 'monster-man sandwiches'.

They would hardly fit into the conventional lunch box let alone someone's mouth but they vanished quickly enough when Philly and Mark arrived.

Some of the opposition players came back as well and found it hard to believe they where still in Dublin given the amount of tractors passing by the pub.

After the Joseph's team had departed we conducted a post-mortem on our progress to date. From the start, we had encouraged everyone involved to give their opinion no matter how harsh.

I believe that 'the man that never made a mistake, never made anything' and we needed the input and goodwill of everyone to try to make it work and establish hurling in the area.

Despite the four point defeat which effectively knocked us out of the championship, everyone remained upbeat that evening,

For Ed that opening game with Setanta would remain a highlight. As he recalled in later years, no one had given us any hope and to have competed against them was a big plus in itself.

'Flats', Peter and myself stayed there until the small hours with business more than pleasure on our agenda as we planned our next course of action.

While four or five of us could never agree on virtually anything, in the end we were always prepared to compromise.

The main item discussed that night was the issue of levies. Wild Geese were a small club and with many of our hurling players already members of other clubs, fundraising was something that was always going to be hard.

From our initial meeting we agreed that adult hurlers would not become a burden on the club. One of the first things we introduced was a €2 levy per player per match to cover the cost of the referee's expenses. That alone provided an annual saving of €600 for the club. In addition, we had lost a fair few sliotars during our first home game that evening and this was a cost we could not sustain, which was why there was a new urgency to get two large nets for behind the goals. We decided to host a pub quiz and the entire club rowed in behind us to help us raise €1600.

This was an important development as we discovered early on, that without a large net behind the goals to catch the sliotars, the car park had become a dangerous place to be.

Ballyboughal GFC kindly donated old street lamp poles for us to hang the new nets on. Kevin Monks and Gerry Fitzsimons secured the poles into the ground and then the nets where erected. The car park became a safer place again. All this had taken place within four weeks.

Due to our late entry in the 2008 Dublin hurling scene, the fixtures from the Dublin County board were very slow in coming. We had a fairly frustrated bunch of new hurlers who wanted to hone their skills and were gagging for games. We decided to borrow Robbie Kelleher's famous saying, taking out the word 'football' and adding hurling, 'that the only way to learn how to play hurling was to play hurling'.

We established relationships with hurling teams of a similar level in the neighbouring counties of Meath, Kildare and Louth. Thus when the other Dublin adult hurling teams were fixed to play and we were not, we travelled.

Our first ever win came on the road in Kilmessan. Meath's most successful hurling only GAA club have 28 county senior hurling titles to their name.

The village is nestled at the bottom of Tara hill, the same spot where Oldtown's Molly Weston and her brothers had lost their lives for Ireland in the United Irishmen rebellion. A 1-14 to 0-14 win over their third team was the result in a hard-fought encounter. It was a notable day also for the performance of Mattie Lambe. That was the first time we saw his true hurling potential. He gave a superb second-half showing, scoring four points from play from his wing-forward position.

Before that game he had not been an automatic selection but he had applied himself diligently in the few short weeks of his hurling life. Mattie was a hard grafter at training and was rarely absent and any advice he got, he took and utilised.

Ed was on holidays in Italy at the time and he was the first to get the text announcing our victory. As we travelled home, the banter was better then usual because we had a win to savour under our belts.

Half-way home we got what would turn out to be a customary text from 'Flanno'. Seemingly they had taken a wrong turn or two and ended up in Skryne in Co Meath. Worse than that though was they had also run out of petrol. And that's why Flanno was texting. We got great fun out of their predicament but then returned to our analysis of the game.

In many ways we had demolished the argument that you must start hurling at a young age. Our defence and midfield was reasonably settled by now. The forward lines fluctuated a lot and any newcomer was instantly tried up front with fingers crossed that he might be the answer to our prayers. We were good at winning possession, holding it and passing but our Achilles heel was in the scoring area. I knew it was the same with most teams in the country and took heart from that thought.

The reality was we were heavily dependent on frees. We worked on shooting points while on the run. The only one at this stage that seemed to be making serious progress was Mattie. That showed us patience was needed if we were to uncover any other gems. We knew one another well and thankfully there was no sign of frustration and the siege mentality of the early days helped us bond. Personally I could read a game better in my head but found that the body could not keep up with my mind. I worked on trying to hone my ability to be in the right place at the right time.

The two Rennies had mastered the skill of free-taking although there was an over-reliance on them.

Playing games every week had helped us to gel and the fixtures we arranged gave all the panellists, about 40 at that stage, plenty of game time.

That September we moved the training indoors as the clubs floodlights were poor. It was Sean Madigan's idea to switch to the indoor complex sited in the Ward, about 4 miles from Oldtown.

For some of the older lads it was an extra strain at times. Between football and hurling, there was little time they could call their own between the training and playing of games.

Training mightn't be as tough maybe in comparison with teams who are playing senior or intermediate football.

Obviously it was of a higher level than what we had at Wild Geese but you have to appreciate that a lot of our fellows were 30 or over which militated against the high level of intensity required.

You could only do what your body allowed you. The training was always going to be skills-based and not physical. As Peter would always emphasise: 'you cannot outrun the sliotar'.

So we actually trained for the whole winter. That was a help to our

The Wild Geese team on that historic first day, the 23rd of May, 2008. There were eight different GFCs represented on this team. We drew 1-9 each. **Back row, left to right:** Martin Flanagan, David McDonald, Paul Flood, Ed Sweetman, Aidan Lenehan, John Rennie, Philly McCarthy, Dave Rennie, Chris Keane, Mark Kealy and Collie Prenderville. **Front row:** Graham Moore, Danny Kelly, Charlie Rooney, Nathan McCaffrey, Sean Madigan, Paddy Jones, Sean Flatley, Tom Smyth, Andy Ryan, Shane Byrne, Richard Daly and Peter McGowan.

ABOVE: Gerry Fitzsimons, Eamon Robinson, Dave Sammon (with his son Daniel in front).
BELOW: Umpire extraordinaire Vincey Fitzpatrick.

ABOVE: Peter Rooney, 94-year-old Wild Geese president Charlie Rooney and Pat Prenderville were in attendance that first day.
LEFT: Paddy Jones, Chris Keane and Tom Smyth warm up as we wait for the referee. Peter and Flats (with the 'big feckin bandage' in the background).

CHAIRMAN OF THE BOARD

Wild Geese chairman Sean McNulty

THE CLASS OF 2009

The 2009 team just before the hard-earned 1-8 to 1-5 victory over Raheny. **Back row, left to right:** Mattie Lambe, Dave Rennie, Ed Sweetman, Aidan Lenehan, John Rennie, Martin Flanagan, Paul Flood, Philly McCarthy, Ciaran Smith, Peter McGowan, Tom Smyth, David McDonald and Collie Prenderville. **Front row:** Danny Kelly, Sean Madigan, Shane Byrne, Arron Creighon, Sean Flatley, Fiac Andrews, Mark Kealy, Nathan Mc Caffrey, Danny Monks and David Reilly.

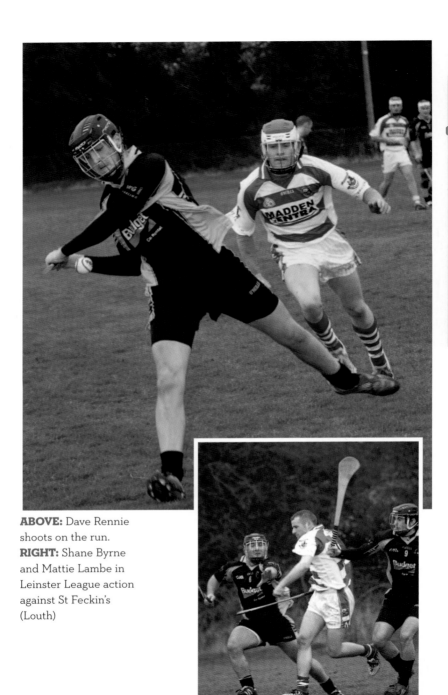

ABOVE: Dave Rennie shoots on the run.
RIGHT: Shane Byrne and Mattie Lambe in Leinster League action against St Feckin's (Louth)

ABOVE: The goal from Dickser (extreme right of the picture) that sent us on to our first ever competitive win against Erin Go Bragh.
BELOW: 'It Takes Two' Nathan McCaffrey in action against Setanta.

CLOCKWISE FROM MAIN PHOTOGRAPH: Setanta captain Breandain O Gearrain being watched by Sean Madigan; the village is black and amber after Tom Smyth is finished with it, just before the final; "This will never be forgotten" - we listen to our captain after we have won 2-6 to 1-2. No silverware present; Peter talks to Shane and a worried Mattie at half-time in the league final.

THE 2010 UNDER-11s

Back row, left to right: Michael Lenehan, Aidan Lenehan (behind) Mark O'Shea, Jack Kinsella, Jamie Clarke, Eoghan Creaby, Liam Monks, Paul Creaby (behind).

Front row: Daniel Sammon, Cristian Keane, Mark Byrne, Tommy Friel, Jeaic Scott.

THE CLASS OF 2010

The 2010 team just before the 0-13 to 1-10 draw with Setanta. By now we are relegated. **Back row, left to right:** Aidan Lenehan, Ciaran Smith, David McDonald, John Rennie, Mark Kealy, Noel Mooney, Philly McCarthy, Tom Kennedy, Paul Kealy and Ed Sweetman. **Front row:** Shane Byrne, Phil Egan, Nathan McCaffrey, Arron Creighon, Kevin Conway, Sean Flatley, Peter Slye, Sean Madigan and Mick Kennedy.

Aidan Lenehan with his wife Joan and son Michael at Aras an Uachtarain.
Inset, 'There's life in the old dog yet!': Aidan takes possession from Setanta's
Liam O'Brien.

sharpness in the New Year. It's a different sort of training indoors but we practised all the basic things.

Training at The Ward was set for Monday nights 8.30 and lasted for an hour. We had to stick with Monday, the only night guaranteed not to clash with the football training. The numbers attending training remained decent, averaging 15 most nights.

The lads paid €5 a session which made it self-financing.

During the games it was obvious to see that most of the Geese players needed two or three touches to control and this was costing us time and time again. The sessions though paid off with fresh air shots and kicking the ball becoming a rarity. Ed's training regime concentrated now almost exclusively on the basic skills like trying to improve our short passing game, block downs, one touch controlling and shooting.

It was a case of doing the simple things over and over again and I know I thought about the wrist work that Christy Heffernan's uncle Bill had preached to me about in my formative days in Kiltormer. He was a travelling salesman, a long-time friend of my mother's family. We saw him a few times every year and he always had nuggets of hurling advice for me.

A member of the panel before he decided to concentrate solely on his football was Fiach Andrews. Fiach was a fine hurler who had played alongside Ciaran Kilkenny at Scoil Chaitríona in Glasnevin and having a famous father was to prove of benefit to us.

Val Andrews had a lengthy coaching career with the likes of the Louth and Cavan while also taking charge of both the Dublin junior and minor teams.

Now Val was not one to stand idly by and so he agreed to take sessions at the Ward on an informal basis.

And while not noted as a hurling expert, his training techniques and ability to make all listen was very welcome. Certainly not many 'bottom-of-the-barrel' teams can claim to have had an inter-county manager train them, even just for a short period. And that someone of his stature could have an interest in a group like us was a pleasant surprise.

Another first was the decision to field an U-21 team that year.

We entered the team into the lowest category level. Although we had Shane captaining and a number of the first team players from the adult team available, we were entering unknown territory.

The U-21 championships are a minefield and it is impossible to predict the quality of the teams you might face.

We had a panel of 15 for this 13-a-side competition which meant we were operating with just a surplus of two and to be honest many of the lads simply were there making up the numbers.

When the fixtures came out we found ourselves in the U-21 D county semi-final against Setanta. Only three teams had entered at this level.

On a November day we hosted the game and started well by going into a 0-2 to 0-1 lead. Then the wheels came off. Dave Rennie, arguably our second most influential player got a foot injury after 10 minutes and had to come off. He was followed off by Jamie Sutton who although wearing a helmet had a received a heavy belt to the head which ended his involvement in the game

Our goalkeeper Danny Monks who had been busy but coping well then let in a soft goal just before the break and before we knew it we where now eight points behind.

Myself and Dicey talked to the team at half-time but I knew and they knew we were beaten. I tried the 'keep the heads up high and keep fighting talk' but unfortunately it didn't work.

Within minutes of the restart Danny had picked the ball out of his net another three times. Shane looked over at me at one stage with an accusing expression, his hands up in the air as in a surrender gesture, as if he wanted to walk off.

I shouted at him: 'What the heck do you want me to do?'

Brother-in-law or no brother-in-law I was in no mood to back down. The game had turned into a shambles and the 30 minutes of the second half was one of the longest of my life.

I didn't know what the final score was and didn't want to know either. The finger had come out of the dam and the flood was massive. The clubs first venture into the U-21 championship had ended in ignominy.

CHAPTER 8
BACK TO THE FUTURE

The manner of our collapse against Setanta reminded us that tough times lay ahead but we were not unduly worried. The seed for underage hurling had already been planted a year before. It was the spring of 2007 and Oldtown native Peter Rooney was knocking on Dave Sammon's front door. He wanted to talk with Dave about trying to get juvenile hurling off the ground in the village.

He had just come from a Wild Geese GAA committee meeting, where the consensus was that the community and club needed something to re-invigorate it. Rooney and McNulty had little hurling experience and while they may not have had any real love for the game they both were smart enough to see the opportunity. It was a niche opening and something that would attract the youth.

Both of them were conscious that Saint Margaret's had tried to start a juvenile hurling section to no avail a few years earlier. In Saint Margaret's case this effort failed to get off the runway.

They felt this new initiative might help galvanise the community. Promoting the national sport was on their minds and in hurling they had something that no other GAA club in rural north county Dublin could offer.

A primary motive in this push was the local rural renewal. In truth there was very little else in the way of entertainment in the village.

Rooney was under no illusions about what the club faced in terms of getting the venture up and running and then sustaining it on a long-term basis.

Peter's mother in fact had played for Oldtown's camogie team in the 1930s. Back then they played in Mooretown which was not far from the family home owned by his father, Charlie, who at 95 is the current Wild Geese president.

A group of lads from Rolestown and Oldtown had formed a hurling team in the 1950s called Fingal Rovers. The team was the brainchild of Tommy Butler, Austin Gleeson and the MacBride brothers. Former Dublin footballer Liam Collins, who resided at the Glebe house in Kilsallaghan, was their full-back. They only survived a few seasons, the untimely death of Butler in an explosion plus retirements were the main factors in the failure.

For a brief period in the late sixties the Wild Geese fielded teams at both under 16 and under 18 levels and at one stage Sean McNulty had played in goals for the fledgling teams.

The team folded but the efforts of manager Gus Warren were not forgotten and today there is a plaque erected to him at the entrance to the pitch.

Their undoing then was a lack of coherent structure and a dearth of experience.

Nonetheless they felt this new venture had a good chance of survival and in David Sammon he had a kindred spirit.

Dave, a native of Kilmacud who had moved to Oldtown after marrying a Cavan woman, was known as an energetic organiser with the juvenile sections at the neighbouring Fingal Ravens GAA club. Many of the Oldtown youths played their football there and he consequently was very receptive to Peter's plan. Soon after, the pair visited the Dublin County board. There they found a very supportive CEO in John Costello. The board gave as much as they possibly could in the way of equipment and the offer of a coach. It's hard to put a figure on it but new helmets are €65 each and they probably came back with 50 helmets. So between juvenile goalposts, helmets, hurls and sliotars, the club got between €3,000 and €4,000 worth of hurling gear.

By having the gear, a major obstacle that could have stopped things from taking off, was eliminated in one fell swoop.

The establishment of the juvenile section, the first ever in the club's 119 year history, was very significant.

Today the Wild Geese are one of the few clubs in Dublin to have a juvenile-only hurling section and in Sammon they had an excellent administrator.

He enlisted some of the local parents as mentors. Flatley was assigned to the under 10s and proved an excellent coach and unearthed a few gems in Sean Dunphy, Dara O'Brien and Mattie King.

Paul Creaby, who coached rugby in Ashbourne RFC as well as Gaelic football in Ravens took charge of the under-8s along with St Gall's man, Gerry Friel.

Encouraging as it was to see non-hurling people getting on board, a lack of experienced coaches with the exception of Sean Flatley and Ed would prove a problem.

However every little helped and the club was also boosted by the arrival of Larry McDermott. He is one of 40 GPOs operating out of Parnell Park (Dublin County board HQ) and was provided as a free resource in a response to the initiative.

His first visit to Wild Geese territory was at Dave Sammon's house to meet Sean McNulty and Dave.

Larry was with his manager Emer Dignam and although a Dubliner, recalls tailing Emer's car around the dark country roads to get to his destination.

McDermott eventually found the place but having met the new mentors for the first time that night he realised he would have to get used to 'hurling' in the dark.

The floodlights are powered by ordinary single-phase electricity, the same as ordinary homes. The floodlights are 12-year-old technology halogen light fittings which when running do not permit the operation of the showers in the dressing-rooms. The lights are based around the top end of the pitch which means the bottom pitch is dark.

This means that everyone gets crowded into the brighter end with very little room to operate.

But as the days grew longer, Larry began to look forward to his drive out to Oldtown, particularly when the weather was good.

The numbers that came in the beginning were high but it levelled out within the first season. Every Wednesday evening the pitch in Oldtown was a hive of activity with an average of 95 juveniles at training.

Based on the four main national schools in the area in 2010, on boys aged 7-12, the penetration rate achieved was 25 per cent.

Within two years, trying to deal with the various levels within each group was very demanding.

As well as training the juveniles the club decided in 2010 to start a camogie team because at this stage the girls had come of age and were no longer allowed to play on mixed teams.

The camogie county board was very supportive with a grant of €1,000 available to them if they wanted it. They had three open sessions but the first coincided with a heavy snowfall in the middle of February 2010.

They had two more open days after that with two coaches – Mary Madigan and Sinead Andrews – who were both very keen and very interested.

Despite this, it was to no avail and the maximum that turned up for either of the two open days was seven.

To be fair I never thought it would work out. If you look at the camogie profile in the general area, there is no team in Swords while the only camogie team north of Swords in Dublin is Skerries Harps.

We owed it to the girls that had stayed and had played hurling for two or three years to give it a try. They had arrived initially to play with Sean Flatley's team and were with the under 10s then.

There was continued encouragement at boys level with a recognition of the importance of playing the game on a regular basis.

The Dublin County board's rotation fixture system means that the games never clash which is a great plus for players wanting to play both codes. At the moment if you go into a number of clubs you see GFC on the gates. The guy with the hurl is also part of the GAA. What are those GFCs saying to the other codes in GAA like handball, like Scor and hurling?

Soccer is the big threat in my estimation and the reason why the alternative football/hurling weekends works is that hurlers are always available for football selection and so steer away from soccer.

Soccer weekly fixtures clash with both GAA codes. It's possible for players to play both GAA codes in Dublin long term with no collision.

The same cannot be said if you mix either code with other games, because you are guaranteed collision.

Of the 91 GAA clubs in Dublin, 43 are dual status but that compares favourably with Cork where 92 of the 165 clubs are dual, Galway where only 10 of the 78 clubs are dual and Roscommon where only 2 of the 27 clubs are dual sports.

But the scope for larger hurling numbers in the capital is there. Our movement has shown that you do not necessarily need tradition of the game in the region to necessarily get it off the ground. Hurling is certainly more difficult then any other game but there's nothing more Irish.

Hurling is in every one of us. My father never played when young but he picked it up and learned the basics.

There is no history of hurling being played in the Fingal area but I am certain that before colonisation it was played all over the country.

And I think this is why it was not a Gaelic football, a soccer ball or a rugby ball that was presented to President Obama or Prince Philip.

CHAPTER 9
COMMITMENT

Our 2008 record showed that we played 23, won one, drew one and lost 21. Nothing to write home about. Yet we received an unexpected honour when we were nominated as Junior hurling club of the year by the Friends of Dublin Hurling group.

Only three clubs were nominated with the winner receiving €1000 which for a small club like ours would have been a God send.

Sean, Peter, John and I went to the awards dinner in the Grand Hotel, Malahide and while we didn't win we got a few honourable mentions.

I realised that evening sitting among the peers and hierarchy of the Dublin hurling scene that it was going to be a rocky road for hurling at the club. We had no serious GAA credentials, the club had never won anything worthwhile in its long history. No golden era. Although one amber beacon was flashing, that went un-noticed by most. The U-11s had just won their league. A club hurling first. Certainly no one could have expected what was around the corner.

The season was over and by now we had stopped training by mid November. The next time we were all together was the Christmas party which was held in Oldtown House pub. Every one was in good spirits although the country's turmoil had just begun and the dark clouds started to circle. Thankfully all the lads were working and were oblivious to it at least for the present time.

It was a good night and we laughed and joked for hours. We were in total agreement that while the year had been fun and progress was made, undoubtedly we were the worst team in the county.

All in all though things were going well and in that first year alone we went through 60 players.

By the end of the season we had about 35 on our books and more importantly we had 20 constantly turning up to train.

Shortly after the end of the festivities, Ed, Sean and I met in

Sean's house. It was a frosty night and we were armed with pens and note pads but did very little writing. We decided to ask David 'Dicey' McDonald to join the management team. He was playing with us and was also a selector on the Wild Geese junior football team.

We felt it would be good to have a direct conduit between the two as it would keep the relationship smooth, especially at this early stage. Dicey was a good trainer and tactician, the latter department being a weak area for us. It was agreed to bring the team back training indoors at the end of the month when the clocks went forward.

We hoped that season to share the running of the training sessions between the three of us and Peter to take some of the burden off Ed and allow him concentrate more on getting himself in shape for the games.

If you take the likes of Ed, myself, Flats, and Sean Madigan we'll never really be truly fit again. Ed, worked on the quays in the city and sometimes it suited him to cycle. Normally Ed would leave home at about quarter to seven and get there just before eight.

It's about 20 miles or 32 kilometres and a lot of that journey back is uphill.

For Ed the big thing was to try. His knees gave him trouble over the years. But as he would say himself: 'It's a self-fulfilling prophecy that as you reduce your weight the load on your knees gets less'.

I had my doubts though myself. I kept telling him the more he is doing to get fit the more he is getting injured.

I think at our age, over 40, you have to pace yourself. I started working hard on my fitness in 2009 and I found the more I did, the more my body was beginning to say that's enough.

Fitness reasons aside, Ed's decision to take a break from doing the coaching made me slightly uneasy as my coaching skills and ability to get my message across paled in comparison to his natural ability. At the same time it was important to be fair and share the load.

We agreed the aim for the season was to win half of our competitive games. No point running before we could walk. That season we were re-graded to the lowest hurling league in Dublin at the time, division

8. (There were 96 adult hurling teams in all), as well as the lowest graded Championship, Junior E.

The latter was the more prestigious of two competitions and would also be the harder to win. That night we decided on Sean Madigan as the captain, as he was as a good listener and great talker. He's very popular among the panel and was to prove an inspired choice.

That said his spell as captain began rather curiously. It was our first training session of the year which coincided with a heavy snow fall.

Despite the weather, it was always important to have a good attendance there for the first night and so dressed in only his togs and jersey he set out for the short journey to the Ward.

Now GAA folk are known as hardy souls who will train in any weather but this did not impress his wife whose parting shot of 'you're mad' could be heard as he departed down the driveway.

And as events transpired, Sean had only got to the top of Killeek lane in St Margarets, a hard place to get out of at the best of times, when his van skidded into the ditch.

So Seán got out of the van and the only option he had was to run up to his brother Hubert's house to get help. Hubert was surprised to see him dressed in his shorts out in the snow at the door.

The two brothers tried pushing the van but got no joy. At this stage more people passed but they were more interested in taking photos and slagging than actually assisting.

Eventually Sean rang 'Flats' to let him know what had happened and why he wouldn't be able to make the first training session. 'Flats' told Sean as if he needed any further convincing that he was mad 'not to worry about it and to go home'. Then in a show of comradeship, 'Flats' accompanied by a few of the Oldtown lads took a diversion and surprised the Madigan brothers on the side of the road. All together they managed to pull the van out of the ditch.

Sean's vehicle emerged with very little damage and while Hubert whose help was appreciated went home to his nice warm fire, the rest with their captain in tow headed for training in a slow moving convoy as the snow continued to pelt down.

Perhaps oblivious to the heroic deeds that happened on Kileek lane, that night Ed introduced a roll call for training in the hope of keeping a little bit of pressure on everyone to attend.

Some of the class of 2008 failed to re-appear, their brief flirtation with hurling was over.

That was not too surprising as from the very beginning, we had lads coming and going all the time. We realised that to commit to a hurling team was not an option for many for various reasons.

But there was still the overall desire by the squad to persist with our national game and that was to be commended.

And we were boosted by the addition of two new players, Aaron 'Gooch' Creighton and David Reilly, both of whom were to make a huge difference.

Both, who were in their late teens, had for a time dabbled with the small ball and were encouraged by Sean Madigan, a clubmate of theirs at St Margaret's to try their hands at it again.

Reilly was in particular a very gifted footballer who could shoot points for fun off either feet and was an integral part of the Margarets side that narrowly missed out on a semi-final play-off spot in Division three under Paul Clarke.

From the off the two blended in immediately.

The downturn in the recession however was beginning to impact off the field for some of our members.

Shane, an apprentice carpenter and Mark Kealy, a bricklayer had lost their jobs. Shane couldn't handle 'the nothing to do and all day to do it' as he was young and always in a hurry.

For Mark Kealy, it was a hard blow particularly given that he and his partner had just taken out a mortgage.

Mark worked along with his brother Paul as bricklayers with a construction company but was to receive notice by letter from their foreman that they were on two weeks notice.

The company eventually went under in May 2011 with debts of €500 million. The lads were offered statutory redundancy of two weeks for every year. After some union intervention that was increased to three and a half weeks for every year. Mark had been there seven years, and Paul three so needless to say their situation was fairly grim at that stage.

The dole offices were now snowed under but the first person Mark met there was Shane. The queue was five hours long and it took three months for Mark's social welfare payments to go through.

So the situation now facing Shane and Mark put everything else into perspective.

We talked about it openly as a group and that first evening we agreed to keep an eye out for job opportunities for the two lads. Their situation was really a shot across the bow as several others were worried about their own occupations. The country only recently at near full-employment, was now witnessing 1,500 people losing their jobs every single day in February of 2009. What a turn around!

The unemployment figure then stood at 326,100, 9.2 per cent. It was the highest monthly increase since 1969 but at least the hurling gave them an escape from the gloom even if only for a few hours a week.

And it was without doubt an advantage to have a united group that got on well together, the various coming and goings never managed to interrupt this. All newcomers were made most welcome.

Following a brief meeting where Dicey was introduced as part of the new management team, we commenced our first game of the new season which was a challenge match against a weakened Donaghmore/Ashbourne side in Oldtown.

We couldn't have asked for a better start when Reilly got possession near the halfway line, soloed down the right wing and planted the sliotar directly over the bar. 'Jesus, it's a miracle' exclaimed one of our substitutes. I nodded and wondered if our prayers had indeed been answered?

And if you were a praying man, then the answer was an emphatic yes.

We won 2-9 to 0-3 with Reilly giving an exquisite performance as we recorded our first ever home win (also our first ever win in county Dublin) and perhaps most significantly it was the first time we had more scores from open play than placed balls.

We could now look forward to the 2009 campaign although our first league game ended in disaster.

While the Dublin County Board runs off hurling and football leagues on alternative weeks, cup games in football fall outside of this.

And with soccer games also scheduled for that day, one of us was bound to lose out.

Now I had no issue with that and actually I expected it but a few losses early in the season could mean it would be over before it even began and then what would the numbers be like at training?

To compound our problems, our opponents, Clontarf, refused our request to move the game and with a weakened team we were heavily beaten by 5-8 to 2-4.

To make matters worse, 'Flanno' got sent off midway through the second half although we could see it coming.

The referee, although quite young, was good. 'Flanno' continually questioned his decisions and in the end the referee had no choice but to send him off.

Morale didn't get any better when we lost away to Greystones in our next game. We had decided in our innocence to enter a team into the lowest level of the Leinster Hurling League, a competition that takes place every spring.

It was open to all Leinster hurling clubs and provided us with a good yardstick to compare ourselves with clubs from other counties.

Sean, however, was less than convinced about the venture and felt that the way our luck was running we would end up drawing some crack outfit from Kilkenny.

In the groups stages of the competition, we played Greystones away, where we actually performed well and fielded a strong team but still lost 2-14 to 0-5.

The gulf in class was a bridge too far for us at that stage of our development. St. Feckins of Termonfeckin came to Oldtown on Easter Monday for the final group match where we lost by eight points. We have not re-entered the Leinster league since but that's more of a reflection on us and not the actual competition.

It was then back to the league where the visit of Clonee side, Erin Go Breagh heralded the initial wind of change.

We actually won with a little bit to spare. This was our first ever competitive victory and Shane jokingly asked after the game: 'Why can't we play them every week'.

Certainly this win showed us what we were capable of if we realised our potential.

The question was – could we do it on a regular basis? Might we have a run now of three or four victories and haul ourselves up the table and into contention for honours? The addition of Gooch and Reilly certainly tipped the balance a bit more in our favour and gave us a greater pick even if the majority of the starting team had been there from the beginning.

We were certainly starting to come together as a team. A big plus for us was that Ciaran Smith was beginning to excel at wing back. Tough as nails, a great man marker and afraid of nothing. The number seven was effectively his.

Beside him Shane at centre-back was showing phenomenal pace and power and by covering his teammates gave us an added measure of assuredness at the back. Off the field, you could sense in the squad a growing worry of the growing economic crisis. In some way, though, it strengthened their resolve.

Mark's job situation had not improved with only the odd bit of temporary work. With us, he had taken over at full-back and by now had made it his position.

Mark's brother Paul also had plenty of time on his hands but after joining us in mid-season, the Wild Geese team became his new focus and soon he had his name on the number two jersey.

The engine of our team was Collie Prenderville. He was like a machine that went on forever. He could zig-zag the pitch without breaking sweat and often went on long solo-runs forward, where he would kick the ball over the bar.

He chose to kick because his confidence with the hurl on the run was quite low. Also he could only hit off one side.

Despite these drawbacks, he was a great asset to our panel. He is a quiet lad both on and off the field, who encourages those around him. No matter how bad the odds are stacked against us he never gave off an aura of negativity. He also was so brave that it rubbed off on others.

Allied with that, he had an eye for the chance and great vision. As a serious athlete who had once been tried out with the Dublin senior football team, he was certainly admired by the rest of the panel.

Overall our teamwork improved by the week and while some mightn't have been always up to the pace, their teammates would invariably go in and help them out.

So heading into a crucial run of fixtures, expectation levels were high.

Then it happened... we won our next three championship rounds on the trot, at home to Civil Service and Na Fianna and away to Kilmacud Crokes.

We scored 17 points and gave an exhibition of decent hurling by our standards against the latter and an away win against Crokes meant a quarter-final berth was secured. Not bad for mid-May. Our momentum was building. The main reason for the turnaround in fortune was that strong team-spirit both on and off the field. We never knew when we were beaten.

CHAPTER 10
CROSSING THE RUBICON

For me the day we crossed the Rubicon was in our league game at home against Raheny on the 23 May 2009.

It was a very significant match because they were a very physical side but the team we put out that day were capable of winning games of that nature.

From the start of the game we knew we were in a battle. They had a very strong trio of players down the middle and gave no quarter.

However once we took the lead early on we never lost it.

It was the type of game that suited us to be honest. Genuine physicality had been one of our strong points and with that came the ability to intimidate. I don't mean by playing dirty, more in terms of physical power to control proceedings.

We are very mindful in the club that guys have to go to work the next day and the reason we all play is to enjoy ourselves. So there was no question of us deliberately trying to injure someone.

But the average height of our full-back line is 6'3" with eight of our starting 15 against Setanta in our debut season over 6'1". I felt if they didn't use their size and their height then they were doing an injustice to themselves

Certainly this helped keep us in that game at crucial times, particularly in areas where our hurling skills were lacking.

When they come up against someone half their size they should easily be able to shoulder him without fouling. I felt that day we had the ingredients to pull off the win even if it took us a while to get over the line.

The defining moment had come early in the second half when Sean Madigan, playing at corner-forward, received an accurate pass from 'Flanno' and headed for the Raheny goal.

He took some serious flak on the way in but as he stumbled between two burly Raheny backs, he managed to tap the sliotar across the line. The enduring image of that moment was Sean McNulty signalling the goal in his capacity as umpire. The roar of delight from the rest of the team could be heard in O'Connell Street.

Ed and Peter ran on with the magic sponge and first-aid kit to the goal scorer but there was nothing in it that would cure him, only time.

We helped him to his feet. He was dazed and staggered the few steps, like a new-born foal before steadying himself and raising his hands, shouting out 'yes' triumphantly.

Nothing could beat us now. The game resumed and while they threw the proverbial kitchen sink at us, this was destined to be our day.

The dressing-room afterwards was like a Crimean slaughter house but it was the happiest one yet.

Sean Madigan needed help to take off his body armour. He was sent some by a cousin in the US years ago, quite unorthodox looking and moth eaten. 'The American footballers wear them and swear by them' he told us and who were we to argue?

Sean, body armour and all, was not the only with battle scars that day.

I had taken a bad blow to the side of my upper body and had some serious pains around my rib-cage. I managed to drive home and drop Joan off at the airport without her noticing my pain.

She was heading to East Cork to do a cookery course and once I was alone I headed straight to the VHI health clinic in Swords.

I was brought into the A and E area and the curtain was drawn. The Eastern European Doctor who examined me thought I had been in a brawl: 'You were fighting?' he asked accusingly. 'No Doc, I was just playing hurling' I replied.

I might as well have been talking double Dutch to him as he didn't understand what I meant.

During the examination, I got a text on my phone. It said: 'I'm beside ya' – from Sean Madigan. It took a few moments to register but when the doctor was finished with me, I peeped behind the curtains to see Sean sitting up on the bed. Before either of us could speak, the doctor returned. 'You two were fighting', he asked accusingly? There was no point in trying to explain to him that it was a hurling match. So we just let it go.

Sean and I chatted for a few minutes before undergoing x-rays. Neither of us had anything broken thankfully and had fully recovered within a few days. The victory was so sweet, nothing could take away from that and the pain was well worth it.

We played Raheny again in April this year and it was another bruising encounter.

There was one incident where I went through and just as I was going to line up a goal, I was taken out.

Our elation over the Raheny victory was short lived. The following day at training, 'Flats' an airline mechanic at SR Technics told us his job had been put on notice. The company were pulling out and all staff where going to be made redundant. You could see the strain on his face. He has a wife, three young children under the age of nine and a mortgage to be paid.

On the first Thursday in June we arrived over to Silver Park in Stillorgan, one of the homes of Kilmacud Crokes with only 16 lads.

While it is officially a 13-a-side league, most elect to play 15-a-side, which we did. This meant though that the injured 'Flanno' was our only substitute. We had won here a month earlier in the championship but this team was a good bit weaker. The pace of the game was fast on the warm summer's evening but we were slow out of the blocks. Fifteen minutes into the second half we were eight points down. A long 'Hail Mary' shot from Philly at midfield was covered by the Crokes 'keeper but in a lapse of concentration, he dropped it across the line.

His confidence in tatters, the following puck-out from him was a miss hit, 40 metres into the hand of the unmarked McCaffrey, who gained some ground before bagging goal number two.

A Lazarus-like resurrection was now on the cards. At the other end 'Flats' kept us in the game with a miraculous save, his resulting clearance found David Reilly. He soloed a bit, then cool as you like, rifled the sliotar into the top right corner of the net.

Neither team could believe what had just happened. The last few minutes were nail biting but we managed to hang on for the narrowest of wins 3-5 to 0-13.

As I walked off the field, I was joined by my cousin Barry Gavigan, the player/manager of Crokes. I consoled him but could not hide my delight. 'That was daylight robbery' I conceded to him.

He agreed wholeheartedly. We didn't deserve to win but having lost to that Crokes team twice in 2008, the unexpected win was welcome.

Confidence is a fragile thing but on this occasion we kept fighting to the end. I couldn't imagine any other sport producing such a turnaround so quickly and needless to say we had a celebratory drink in Kettles, the local hostelry in Rolestown, when we got back.

CHAPTER 11

THE VISITATION

Soon after that game I got a call out of the blue from RTE's Sean O'Brien of 'The Sunday Game.' He told me that our adult hurling team had been chosen to receive a two-hour training session which would be filmed, edited and screened at a later date on the programme

As part of the GAA's 125 year celebrations, there were four clubs chosen across the country, two in football and two in hurling. We were the only Leinster club to be picked and certainly I think the fact that most of the lads had just taken up the game was a big selling point in terms of the proposal we sent in.

When it was announced that Ger Loughnane was taking the session I was ecstatic. I knew with Ger there it would be just a totally positive experience for the whole club and community.

I consider Ger Loughnane to be a national treasure. A two-time all star as a player for Clare in a playing career that spanned 15 years, he subsequently managed Clare to two All-Ireland successes in 1995 and 1997. And the emotion witnessed after the 1995 victory (the banner county's first All-Ireland in 81 years) has not been repeated since.

In later years he managed Galway but could not repeat the success and some may argue Clare were primed for success when he took over. Certainly the team and backroom staff had some strong personalities whose infectious enthusiasm would rub off on other counties.

Anthony Daly was the captain of the Clare team in 1995 and has guided Dublin to their first Division One league title since 1939. He is a great leader and has helped rejuvenate the fortunes of the sport in the capital.

Davy Fitzgerald was another who enjoyed success as manager with Waterford before returning to Clare for the season just finished where he ended a four-year winless run in the championship.

Both were determined characters but that 'never-say-die' attitude was no doubt instilled in them by Loughnane.

Loughnane after watching Tipperary's 18 point humiliation of Clare in the 1993 Munster final from the stands, had vowed to wipe the smile of Nicky English's face after he had spotted the former Tipp legend grinning as he drove over a point for the Premier county.

Loughnane would make good on that promise two years later. He went on to become a top class, if sometimes controversial manager and more recently a panellist on the Sunday Game.

Nonetheless his brutally honest interpretations of the game and its various characters have made him a legend in my book.

The fact that nearly a quarter of Liam McCarthy contenders this decade were managed by lads who made their name under Loughnane speaks volumes for his enduring influence.

That call from RTE anyway was to galvanise the community with Sean McNulty convening a special meeting of the club committee.

The following Saturday was designated as a 'clean up day'.

It was a case of all hands on deck, or almost all, for the painting and cleaning. Even Ciaran Smith's heavily pregnant wife Martina, did her bit.

Ger's visit, however, seemed to take years off Oldtown as the whole village got a sprucing up while the town name signage was washed and the streets swept. The excitement in the build-up was incredible.

It was a particularly proud day for Charlie Rooney who supported us through thick and thin since our inception.

An honorary president and a former footballer at the club, Charlie had crammed a lot into his 90 plus years. My own son could not get over the fact that Charlie lived through two world wars and could vividly remember 'the emergency.'

The name Rooney continues to this day in the club with Peter's son, Charlie, now playing with the senior hurlers.

For Charlie snr who had seen the Wild Geese club go through some low times, this was a night worth waiting for with the club now a hive of activity for both young and old.

He told me that the rejuvenation of the club brought about by the hurling, made him extremely proud to be a member of the Wild Geese. In turn I can say he was a great source of inspiration for us.

He would always arrive on time for the games and would position himself near our substitutes.

There he would take in the whole game while only ever offering words of encouragement. Now and then he would venture into the home dressing-room to congratulate or commiserate with us.

Undoubtedly seeing Ger Loughnane inside our hallowed grounds gave him immense satisfaction. It was as if his arrival was an endorsement of the hard work we were doing in terms of raising the profile of hurling in the area.

Ger's arrival on a Tuesday evening coincided with a terrific spell of fabulous warm weather. As he pulled into the car park, the first thing he said was: 'Howya lads, I see you're getting tar.'

We looked at one another and grinned. The car park had been extended earlier in the year and while some hard-core gravel dressing had been put on it there was no tar on the way. We just hadn't the money.

Sean McNulty was first to meet him although Peter Dunphy would make the directors cut as he was filmed shaking the great man's hand. The session was filmed by RTE and the production team who arrived two hours before Loughnane did a brief tour of the town. A lot of filming was done which was eventually edited to a few short minutes.

It was all done in brilliant sunshine and the intensity of heat along with the smell of the fumes from our newly-painted dressing-rooms still remain with me.

The local papers reported Ger's visit which meant about 250 spectators ventured to the pitch for the few hours with some even bringing picnics.

Nearly all the players attended with only two of the panel Mattie and 'Flanno' unable to make it.

Ger began his session with us out on the pitch with a simple, but great opening line: 'Now lads above all this evening we want to have a bit of fun'.

His message was: 'Every time you come to hurling, once you have a ball and a hurley that's all you need'.

The session began with a bit of hand-passing with the emphasis on twisting. 'Twisting all the time'.

It was high-octane stuff with Ger at one stage joking: 'Mind your hands, Tommy Walsh might be around.'

Loughnane singled out Kilkenny defenders for their less than conventional tactics – one of which was to give their opponents a little "wrap on the knuckle' which after a while could wear their markers down.

Tactics like this, which Loughnane felt had gone un-policed by some officials, had again come to the fore in 2009 after Dublin had played Kilkenny in the Leinster final.

There was great merit in his comments with regard to players protecting themselves.

Many of the lads who came into training at first without the basics didn't know how to protect themselves from the blockdown.

They also got belted with an opponent's hurl because they didn't know how to position themselves. Thus a lot of them went home with bruised knuckles.

There was one instance where one of the younger lads got a belt on the arm but instead of blocking his man he turned on him. Unfortunately he didn't understand at the time how to use his hurl to protect himself.

Players need to take on board pieces of advice like this in practice to heighten their enjoyment of the game. Loughnane's session was a real eye opener on the night and we were hanging out of his every word.

'I was watching as you came out on to the field and most began by trying to hit a big haymaker, a Tiger Woods shot trying to get the sliotar to travel the length of the field. Lads, how many times do you hit a ball 100 yards? Goalies do but nobody else. It's all about control, 20 yard or 30 yard passing, that's plenty'.

Ger continued: 'If you can pass 20 yards accurately, that's fantastic'. He got us to do some hand-passing drills and then drills using the hurls in close quarters with the emphasis on soft touches. He talked to some lads individually like Andy Ryan, giving them little insights and tips.

His favourite word was 'faster, faster', that word echoed around North County Dublin that evening. We now knew the training we had been conducting was sufficient but not the tempo or the intensity.

The two hours absolutely flew and it was a thoroughly enjoyable evening. At the end he called us into a circle, thanked us and complimented us on 'our level of skill and great spirit'.

Afterwards, we retreated to the newly refurbished dressing-rooms and on the way he posed for photographs and signed autographs; he had time for everyone, young and old, a very pleasant man and much different from the image he sometimes portrays on television.

Over a cup of tea and a sandwich he admitted: 'Your skill levels were way above what I had expected, if there was a junior E down in Clare, you would think they wouldn't be able to hit the ball'.

Overall it was a very worthwhile experience and we always advise members past and present to take a look at that footage which is available to watch on you tube.

CHAPTER 12
ILLUSIONS
OF GRANDEUR

In the aftermath of Ger's visit a sort of feelgood factor lingered for some time.

Looking back there was nothing that he said in particular that stood out. He just reiterated what needed to be done whether you were playing at junior or county level. First and foremost do the simple things right.

Just keep your eye on the ball. The big thing you had to do was win your own ball and when you had that done you were part of the team.

And if you put that into practice, the team you were playing against regardless of how good they were would struggle to break you down.

As we congregated at Kettles for our next competitive fixture his words were still fresh in our minds.

We departed from the meeting point in various cars. It was just over a year since we began our journey. Myself and Peter Dunphy chatted quietly away in the front of the car, with the odd intervention from his son Sean and Shane Byrne, in the back.

Shane was quiet, still fuming that he got two penalty points and a €80 fine, coming back from Tipperary the previous day with a car load of hurls. The garda searched his car and only when they discovered the hurls did their gentler side appear although by then the garda, a St. Mark's GAA clubman, (who are based in South Dublin) had already written the ticket.

Among the hurls, Shane had two 38' inch sticks, special orders for Philly (incredibly both got broken in the same game in 2012) and you have to remember that the normal size is 34, 35 or 36.

We reckoned the bigger the hurl the easier it was to block but the garda who was also a hurler, went to examine the hurls individually before asking Shane, when he saw the two 38s 'if he had found Fionn McCumhaill?'

This hadn't lightened Shane's mood and as he sat quietly at the back, myself and Peter wondered how best to use Ger's visit to our benefit.

We agreed that we didn't lack ambition but we had to stay realistic and grounded. Peter talked about several clubs in Kilkenny now hurling at senior level who were once junior. Ballyhale Shamrocks and O'Loughlin Gaels had spent most of their existence until recent times in the junior ranks.

He is a big admirer of Brian Cody and particularly his ruthlessness when it came to wielding the axe if a player doesn't come up to scratch.

It turned out that our game with Civil Service was the last for one of our players. As we approached the city centre that morning there seemed no let up in the soaring temperatures with the balmy hot weather still with us.

Apart from a small number of people who were queuing for the zoo, there was barely a sinner to be seen. As we came through Parkgate Street, there was an eerie stillness about the place, like the calm before a storm.

The game was in Islandbridge which was beside the war memorial gardens. The pitch sat on a former rubbish dump, which probably explained its unusual height in relation to its surroundings and possibly for its poor crop of grass. But the first thing that really struck me as I got out of the car was the heat.

We had won our previous three league games and were hoping that we could keep the momentum going, as winning was still a relatively new phenomenon for us.

Civil Service were an unusual concoction with not a Dublin accent among them. They resembled a multi-coloured swap-shop as they had different colours socks and shorts.

That day they had two number 10s which is what one expects in the lowest level I guess.

Being newcomers we read the Dublin County Board rules and comply with the regulations on uniformity of socks and shorts, not wanting to suffer a €50 fine.

Before we last played them they asked to change the fixture from Sunday to Monday. We agreed but were subsequently over-ruled by the Dublin County board.

I later heard rumours that some Civil Service players still playing with other GAA clubs down the country as well and that why weekend fixtures did not always suit them.

I was relieved in a way to be playing a team not at 'full strength' as it allowed us the chance to build on our momentum.

It was their second team we were playing and the omens were good given that we had beaten them at home in the championship earlier on in the season by eight points.

That day we had an embarrassment of riches to pick from and probably the strongest panel turnout ever.

And while there was no evidence that anyone had been out socialising the night before (as it transpired we would never win a game fixed on Sunday mornings until August 2012) the heat was a big issue on the day.

Right from the start we looked a pale reflection of our recent form. Any illusions of grandeur from Ger's visit had been shattered into tiny pieces within minutes of the start.

Say what you like about Civil Service but they could hurl! We were leaking goals, like water in a sieve, while it was mayhem up front, with the forwards falling over themselves.

We won enough possession and made the space but shot lots of bad wides. Half-time came and temperatures began to boil over.

'Flats' and Peter and myself tried calming the lads and pointed out that if you allowed for the soft goals we had conceded and the eleven wides we had accumulated, we were the better team- it just wasn't reflected in the score.

Peter reminded the lads about the Kilmacud Crokes championship game were we had trailed by a similar margin.

'We stuck with it, did not panic and we came right at the end.' It was a taller order this time and you could see that reflected in the faces as they listened, while sipping some water. And as we returned to the field, I doubted if his message had got through.

From the throw in Civil Service dropped a ball in the direction of our goals which their full forward doubled on into the back of the net.

Moments later we had a close call, when their 65' was missed by all and smacked off the cross bar with a loud thump. The trip switch had flipped.

At this stage, Peter had had enough and took myself and Sean Madigan off. We couldn't quibble as we had been anonymous.

'Flanno' and Gooch were introduced. It was our last throw of the dice but almost immediately a 'Flanno's tackle resulted in a free.

Words were subsequently exchanged with the referee, prompting the match official to brandish a yellow card to 'Flanno' while also moving the free forward into a much more scoreable position.

'Flanno' wasn't prepared to let it go though and was still bitching when the referee warned him. 'Another word' he said and you're off as he pointed to the line.

'Mouthing and indiscipline, Jesus, that's that last thing we need' I agreed with Peter.

In the midst of all this turbulence, Ed, at corner back was shouting something to us on the line. 'I think he wants to come off' said Charlie, a sub beside us.

A goal from John Rennie, gave us some hope. Civil service were beginning to wither. They were an older team and it was approaching 30 degrees as we got close to midday, so we were still in with a chance.

Indeed we were beginning to claw back the deficit but 'Flanno' who it seemed had no 'off' switch that day, was soon at it again. Squabbling with the referee for no reason, it was disrupting our potential for a comeback.

Ed gestured to the line again. Peter sent on Charlie Rooney in his place. Ed comes to the line 'I didn't mean take me off, I meant take 'Flanno' off,' he said angrily.

Ed then roared at 'Flanno' to keep his mouth shut and got 'the fingers' as a reply. Ed and 'Flanno' had always had a toxic relationship from day one but now it was becoming open warfare.

But this was not the time or the place and I could see some of our lads on the field looking over to us. Certainly they had enough on their plates without this carry on.

In the end we lost by four points on a scoreline of 4-6 to 2-8.

Straight after the whistle 'Flanno' headed straight for Ed, who stood his ground.

'Oh God, this cannot be happening' I thought.

With both well over six foot they squared up to each other but thankfully there was no physical violence. Peter and I managed to break them up.

Eventually, 'Flanno' walked straight to his girlfriend's car (she had witnessed the whole thing) while Ed headed straight for the dressing-rooms afterwards.

No one knew where to look and the atmosphere in the dressing-room was quite sombre.

It emptied quickly and quietly as everyone mulled over the nightmare scenario that had just unfolded before us. On the journey home, not much was said.

Peter analysed the game explaining that we had 20 wides and should have won. 'Tell me something I don't already know,' I replied.

I was worried about the potential fall-out for the team and hoped that it was not a fatal blow. Both players were held in high regard by the panel and I didn't want it to affect the team morale.

As we passed by the Zoo, the queues were miles long and swelled by dozens of Westmeath fans who could be identified by their maroon jerseys.

They were in the capital for their Leinster semi-final game with Dublin, smiles all over their faces. 'Lambs to the slaughter,' muttered Shane rather prophetically from the back seat with Dublin winning by a whopping 27 point margin.

Still the next day at training, the row was the only topic being discussed. Neither of the lads involved were there. Ed phoned me to tell me he had pulled a muscle and needed to rest it. 'Flanno' was also noticeable by his absence. As it turned out, he never darkened our door again.

CHAPTER 13
ZEROS TO HEROES

It was obvious from the very beginning of our adventure that 'Flanno' had a loathing of authority.

From his early days as a junior footballer with Ravens, he had built a reputation that did not rub off kindly with certain match officials.

Still he was a very talented player and I think if it hadn't been for that most managers would have told him to pack his bags.

His style of play reminded me of Brendan Lynskey, the Galway centre-forward of the eighties. Like Lynskey, 'Flanno' could mop up the breaking ball all day, run with it, take hits and distribute accurately. Not a great scorer but a great man to distribute the ball. The ideal No 11. But unlike Lynskey, when he took the hits he often tended to retaliate. I soon realised he was 'a wanted man'. He had form and some referees were just waiting for the latest outburst.

Martin had an unusual relationship with most people really.

You could see it in Ravens sometimes. A regular feature at midfield under Mick Deegan, 'Flanno' was popular with his Raven's teammates despite the odd outburst. I got on well with Martin and still do but I could never read him, not knowing what he was going to say or do next. He was not the kind of guy you could take under your wing.

I do not know why but sometimes when he put a jersey on he often seemed to go berserk. A lot of time Martin would see a red mist during a match and you couldn't talk to him for love or money.

He had a serious discipline problem. It was tragic because he was really a talented player.

Off the field he was straight up and he said things exactly as he saw it. Black is black and there was no in-between.

Thankfully there was no Saipan type fall-out following his departure.

Martin and Ed were strong characters and I had gone for a policy of non-intervention. It was a case of 'what will be, will be' and I advised others to do the same.

Nonetheless it was discussed briefly among the team and after training Mark and myself lingered on for a bit,

'It was a shame it happened, 'Flanno' is a good player. Wouldn't it be great if they sorted it out?' Mark said.

'Not likely' I replied. While this may have been hard for Mark and maybe others to hear the reality was that Ed and 'Flanno' were like chalk and cheese.

There was a worry 'Flanno's' on-field antics would bring the Wild Geese into disrepute and as a small club still finding its feet, it was something we could do without.

Added to that, I got the feeling that Martin was starting to get a bit restless. He was starting to break back into the Ravens first team and after we had left him off the starting 15 for a cup game against Na Fianna, I remember him remarking 'I didn't give up training (with Raven's) to put up with this carry-on.'

In any case a line was drawn under it soon afterwards, when prior to the start of a friendly with Donaghmore-Ashbourne, Ed called us in for a huddle and apologised for his part in the bust-up.

The friendly had been arranged a few hours before as St. Peregrines had handed us a walkover after being unable to field a team.

It was two more points secured and after we had named the team and brought them up to date with proceedings, I upped the ante by saying: 'The league is there to be won by us.'

Setanta at this stage were runaway leaders but we could take second if we won our remaining league games.

Anyway with the 'Flanno' affair put to bed and having moved on, we went on to win the game 1-10 to 0-10. It proved a good fillip if a brief one as our next game against Commercials was our last group game of the championship – and it didn't end well.

Perhaps typical of Irish weather the sweltering heat of our game with Civil Service had been replaced by a deluge of rain shortly before we took to the Rathcoole Pitch.

It may have been late July but it was a cold and miserable start to the game which we lost on a 4-7 to 1-11 scoreline.

And while we were already through to the quarter-finals, a win there would have given us a potentially easier pairing.

We continued to make strides in the league where we registered four more points with both St Joseph's/O'Connell boys and Na Fianna both conceding walkovers.

Against the latter we travelled up as scheduled to their grounds in Glasnevin on Sunday morning only to be told they could not field a team.

It was disappointing given we had left early from Oldtown and had togged out and had got warmed up before being given the news.

We were determined not to let the morning go to waste and got in a training session there and then. However more trouble was brewing on the horizon.

Up next was a championship quarter final away to St Patrick's Palmerstown's second string. On foot of our recent stint on TV, I received a text from their team coach Ned Rushe enquiring if we were bringing Loughnane with us. If only!

We all met at Kettles as usual and the first one I saw was Shane who even at just five metres away looked a fright. What's up with you' I asked although I already half-knew given that he had been on a lads' week away in Santa Ponsa.

'Food poisoning,' he replied.

'Ya right, booze more like it,' I commented, barely containing my annoyance. We had a strong 15 for the game but this was a bad start to the day.

I had had my clashes with Shane during the years and probably put him under a bit too much pressure to become available at a time when he also had soccer commitments with Swords Celtic.

But I wanted to win every match and put the best team out. And a below par Shane, who had turned in some terrific displays, certainly diminished our chances.

The lads knew that too. If you have three or four lads that are committed and the others see that well then it helps to bring the others in. He was one of the leaders among the lads on the field.

I was mindful never to overstep the mark with the players but also had ambitions for the team and a win in the championship would certainly feed those ambitions.

As we turned off the N4, we found the St Patrick's clubhouse and pitches in Glenaulin Park which is fenced into a small area in a large Dublin Corporation Park.

The grass was very long which was not good for ground hurling while we were not helped by the presence of a gale force wind which Pat's had elected to play with.

Pat's were ahead by 2-4 to no score after 10 minutes.

Midway through that spell, Shane was clearly not up to it and was duly called to the line; a huge loss for us. The holiday had caught up with him.

By half-time Pat's had a firm grip on the game. They seemed to possess talents we lacked and old failings began to surface again with the team heavily dependent on frees to stay in touch.

We showed a lot of heart in the second-half but even with the breeze and Dave Rennie's accuracy from placed balls, it was not enough.

A goal from Dicey at the very end, put a better gloss on the final score of 4-6 to 1-10. A nice touch from Pat's afterwards saw Liam Rushe, who had only just broken on to the Dublin team, come into our dressing-room to wish us luck for the future.

After Liam left, I had to admit I was not that disappointed in the greater scheme of things. We had been beaten by the better team and had achieved one of our goals of reaching the knock-out stages of the championship – not bad for a team of rookies who had just taken up the game.

We still had it all to play for in the league and if we managed to remain unbeaten in our last three league games, we could get promoted and qualify for the league final.

First up were Whitehall Colmcilles and as they were in second place at the time, this was a real four pointer.

It was a very tense affair which saw the two teams finish on 2-12 apiece. They kept coming from behind to level; we felt cheated but it was our own doing. It was a game I felt we could have won but morale was high and numbers at training was still very high.

That evening we got a new recruit called Mick Kennedy, a local national school teacher originally from Enniscorthy. He had played before, years ago and slotted in very quickly. And it was evident from the start that he was a reliable and sound lad.

With the Commercials league game not until early November, we continued our warm-up for what would prove a big month for us.

Ed conducted the training sessions with renewed vigour.

Thankfully Commercials who had handed us a heavy beating in the championship gave us a walkover as they had nothing to play for.

Shortly after the awarding of the points, I rang Sean: 'Jesus, we are within one win of promotion and a league final'.

We arrived in Popintree on 15th November, knowing a win against Setanta and nothing less would secure promotion and a league final berth the following Sunday against the same opposition.

We had never beaten them and while Setanta had already reached the final and gained promotion, they were giving it everything from the start.

We settled quickly into the game with points from Collie and John Rennie with a somewhat fortuitous goal from Shane giving us a two point lead at the break.

During the interval Sean Madigan got us to form a circle and as he slowly moved the full 360 degrees, he uttered in a bellowing tone the immortal lines: 'No one is going to remember us if we get beaten'.

We returned fully-charged up by Sean's rousing speech but Setanta who were aiming to protect their unbeaten run were ready for us and with 10 minutes to go, were five points up.

It looked like an insurmountable lead and I wandered if we had the heart and fighting spirit to pull this game out of the bag. We began to slowly eat away at their lead courtesy of a series of frees from David Rennie. Collie proved the big game changer for us and that terrific sense of timing that had served him so well for Fingal Ravens and the Dublin junior footballers came to the fore once more.

A huge presence at midfield, he set up the crucial run of the game.

He burst through the Setanta defence before unleashing a fierce strike that the 'keeper could only parry.

And fate was to smile on one lucky general, as Napolean would have described it, with the ball landing right at my feet.

For a split-second though time seemed to stand still, before I rifled the sliotar to the back of the net.

Goal!

Almost immediately the referee Tommy Kehoe blew for full time. We had won in the most dramatic fashion and were genuinely shell-shocked.

We had come from nowhere and secured promotion and a league final place in our first full season.

For a team that emerged to fill a hurling void in a quiet remote village in Fingal, this was a major milestone in our lives. I just wanted to run home to tell my wife and son. As we headed for the dressing-room, a smiling Collie caught up with me. 'There you go,' he said.

Collie had always reckoned that heart and spirit, mixed with recklessness had always been the key to our success against teams we had no right to beat. And who was I to argue with that.

Talking afterwards to the Breandáin Ó Greagain, I could see that the Setanta captain was not happy.

A Gaelgoir with a mother from South Africa and a father from Francis Street, he obviously possessed a very competitive streak.

He is a chef very much in the Gordon Ramsay mould and took his game very seriously.

And given that he had the chance to take Collie out in that last eventful solo, I was mindful to choose my words with Breandáin.

'Disgusted, we let ourselves down' he muttered as he made our way off the pitch.

'Ah sure there's always next week,' I said in reply.

'Too right, a chara' he replied.

CHAPTER 14
• • • • • • • • • • • • • • • •
MUCK AND SHITE
AND GLORY
• • • • • • • • • • • • •

The dressing-room afterwards was a happy place but the question was – could we keep it going for one more game?

As a few of us congregated in the car park, we wondered would Setanta be able to bounce back after such a dramatic defeat.

Losing so late on in the game had clearly left them in a devastated state and given our run of late, the momentum certainly seemed to be with us.

It had been our first win over them and Setanta hadn't suddenly become a bad team overnight.

Ed, already looking ahead to the following year, wondered if we were ready to step up the hurling ladder so soon. It was something we hadn't really considered at that stage.

We were determined to enjoy our time in the sun after being a little in the shade with our footballers.

They had finally won the Junior E Championship for the first time in the club's 121 year history and the village was covered in black and amber flags..

With bunting and flags already up everywhere it was decided to leave them for a few more weeks. So no pressure on us there then!

It was a nice pressure to have and there was more good news when 'Flats' informed us that he was one of the lucky SR technics mechanics to get transferred over to Aer Lingus's line maintenance department.

It was a huge relief for himself and his family but it was a very close run thing. Of the 1150 workers, only 96 survived the cut with Sean the last one selected for the transfer. He summed it up thus: 'The door hit me on the back of the head from the inside as it closed'.

Meanwhile Philly had just been let go from the construction company where he had been employed as an electrician.

He managed to stay positive and attended loads of interviews including one for the gardening section of B&Q.

'It was going well, I felt the interviewees liked me,' Philly explained.

Philly told us how he suggested that they put him in the electrical section where he would be of more use but it raised a few eyebrows.

'Philly you shouldn't have said that. Take what you can get, even if it doesn't make sense,' one of us replied.

He didn't get the job and neither did Shane who had applied for a job in the Irish army.

However he was rather taken back when one of his interviewees suggested that the only reason he had applied was because his carpentry apprenticeship had stalled.

A tongue-tied Shane had no answer for that and was not called back. Now both were staring into a long winter of discontent. And what a winter it was.

November of 2009 was to set new met records for the high rainfall and consequent flooding experienced in Dublin and other parts of the country. An Atlantic depression was parked overhead for what seemed like an eternity and not even a friendly wink from RTE's resident weatherman Gerard Fleming could put us out of our misery.

So our league final, provided the pitch was playable, would be a welcome relief for many.

Needless to say, we had the biggest turn-out ever at training the Monday before the game with a strong panel to choose from.

The only real worry for us was that Fingal Ravens had their last league game fixed for the same time. It was a great vote of confidence when both Mattie and Collie texted me to say they were available for selection.

I was later to hear that the Ravens selectors were disillusioned with the choices the two lads made but it was the only time that hurling won out when clashing with the other codes.

Mattie and Collie were now pencilled in but Sean Madigan was a real injury doubt and we were now in a race against time to get him fit. Tom Smyth had heard about our predicament and said he might be in the position to help.

'Work away,' I said. 'It would be a shame not to have Sean for the game.'

Tom collected Sean, telling him he had an ice bath booked for him although no more information was forthcoming.

How effective ice baths are in terms of recovery remains open to question.

Sean, however, was about to experience something completely different. Being carted off to Slane was something he already found strange but it wasn't until they pulled in a farm yard, that he realised the iced-water that awaited him was in a horse bath.

Borrowing the slogan from the old Master card Slogan, Tom would state afterwards: 'The look on Madigan's face was priceless.'

While Tom may not have been on Sean's Christmas card list that year, it did the trick and by the end of the week he was feeling better.

Mark Kealy was away on holiday so we had opted to put Philly in as full-back with Mark's brother Paul drafted into the corner-back position.

As the game drew nearer, I realised that our win over Setanta was covered in luck and felt they would be out for revenge. The game was fixed for their ground and a big home crowd was expected. It was the first time their second team had achieved notable success.

On top of that one of their two mentors, Mark Comiskey had tragically died of a heart attack earlier in the year. He was only 39 and I felt they would want to win badly to honour him.

It was appropriate in many ways that it was Setanta that stood between us and our first piece of silverware.

They had progressed from a juvenile hurling-only club in the 1980s to an intermediate team and their first team narrowly missed out on senior status in September of 2012. There was also a junior E team while their underage structure remained strong.

In short, they are a club we aspire to emulate.

Coming from a predominately football area much like ourselves I hope that in 30 years time we will have an equally good intermediate team.

Setanta benefitted somewhat from the decision of Ballymun Kickhams to concentrate exclusively on football from 1995; the same year that Dublin had defeated Tyrone in the All-Ireland final

Many of those who had played hurling with Kickhams then transferred over to Setanta. They were notable as a club in that it took its early members from the all Irish speaking primary school of Scoil an Tseachtar Laoch and all their early training was given exclusively 'as Gaeilge'.

Setanta was something positive in a community that I felt had received something of a raw deal particularly in terms of its portrayal in the media.

On the day of the game I received an early call from Liam O'Brien, their manager to fix a time for a pitch inspection as it had rained a lot overnight. As I pulled into their car park, I could see a number of their people working on the pitch in a bid to have it right for the throw in.

Liam and myself walked it together. We found that the centre was okay but the top corner was only middling and the goalmouths were very wet with a lot of surface water. I had played on worse but that was scant consolation. The heavy rain had gone but the strong winds were still blowing although this had helped to dry out some parts of the pitch.

We both felt the designated referee, Tommy Keogh, would be likely to pass it if we were happy to proceed. Liam had a plan B. He had the Ballymun Kickhams all-weather pitch booked for the same time just as a precaution. That worried me. A fast pitch would not suit us and we had never played hurling on Astroturf before. I rang Sean, Mattie and Shane for their opinions. I filled them in and asked the question: 'Astro turf or muck and shite'? Without hesitation, the three choose the latter. I told Liam that I would see him back here in a few hours. Fingers crossed the heavy rain would stay away for a while.

More excitement was on the way for at that very moment the Wild Geese footballers were playing a cup final in Garristown where Ciaran had got into a bit of a tangle with his marker during the game. He was already on a yellow and when he resurfaced, he saw yellow again. As he walked to the line, he immediately thought: 'Shit, that's rules me out of the hurling final'.

The first wind I got of it was when Dicey phoned me. 'We won but Ciaran got two yellows, he's devastated, he thinks he cannot play in the hurling final. Can he?'

This was the last thing I needed to be dealing with on the day of a final.

I genuinely didn't know what the story was over Ciaran's eligibility and to get a definitive answer from a county board official on a Sunday morning was a non-runner.

'Listen, let's forget we ever had this conversation. See you in Ballymun at half one,' I said. And there we left it.

The atmosphere in the dressing-room was serious but calm and everyone sat around quietly as we named the team. No surprises in the selection. Ed probably would have got the nod ahead of Paul Kealy to start at corner back in terms of his experience but volunteered to stay on the line.

Then Sean Madigan stood in the middle of the dimly-lit room, looked around slowly and sincerely to his teammates, his friends. He gave a passionate speech and his final words reinforced the view that 'our time had come' – the hairs stood on the back of my neck as I listened. You could hear a pin drop. You could see the togetherness and spirit on the faces. We had not come to lose!

It was blustery as we jogged out to the field, but for now the rain had given us some respite.

Occasionally, the sun would peer through the clouds but overall conditions were challenging for a stylish game of hurling which suited a team of our capability.

This had all the hallmarks of being a close match but few would have expected the outcome. We made a far more convincing start playing with the breeze to take an early two-point lead through two Dave Rennie frees.

Michael Kelly replied with a point for Setanta but on 15 minutes John Rennie scored a goal for the Geese, a rasper of a shot from 10 metres to the top left hand corner of the net, giving their goalie no chance.

Setanta were unhappy not to have got a better return on their scoring chances but with only four points between us at the break 1-2 to 0-1, they were still well in the game.

We were now just 30 minutes away from victory and Peter and Ed encouraged us to remain calm and finish the job.

With the wind at their backs, Setanta erred seriously by switching their centre-back and inspirational captain, Brendan Ó Gearráin to centre forward.

He had been their most effective player in the first-half and we had only scored once from play in that period with the breeze.

He broke up attack after attack and now he was to become the marked man. Shane, our centre-back, was giving a master class and instantly neutralised Ó Gearráin. Besides his phenomenal pace and power, he was always there to cover his teammates.

This was a collective effort and slowly but surely we began to pull away with a Nathan McCaffrey point coupled with a few points from David Rennie.

Setanta replied with a point to raise hopes among the locals of a fighting revival. But a brilliant solo goal from substitute David Reilly put out that flame and while they mustered a goal near the end, time was running out for them.

By now the lads could sense victory with Philly and Paul in jovial mood. Although eight points up, Flats pulled them up by shouting: 'The time for celebrating is after the final whistle'.

Nonetheless you couldn't begrudge the two the moment of glory.

We had the bit between the teeth and nobody had pulled out of the tackle.

Shortly afterwards, the ref blew for full time and for the second time in the week, Setanta had tasted defeat.

For the record, we won 2-6 to 1-2; the victory was more comprehensive than the scoreline suggests.

There was no Dublin county board official on hand with a trophy or no trophy to present to us. I found this to be a bit of an anti-climax as the silverware is normally the focal point. So we were robbed of our few minutes of glory. As Shane put it afterwards it felt like just another 'hurling game in Ballymun.'

Now some might say that the absence of a trophy was as much a reflection of the low standing of the league. The point is we pay as much of an affiliation as the lads in the top divisions. I subsequently learned the cup had been lost a few seasons previously and never replaced.

If I had known that, I would have borrowed a decent sized cup from somewhere, said nothing and kept it in the boot of the car to have in case of victory, for presentation purposes and celebratory purposes only.

Regardless, we savoured the moment. We had come a long way in a few short months, certainly some might say lady luck shined on us more than once or that we just grabbed our chance.

Throughout the season, the teamwork showed every week. And that along with the decision to move our training sessions to the Ward certainly seemed to have made the difference at the end of the year.

Foremost in our thoughts was Mark Kealy who we texted the result to after the game.

The reply showed he too had been busy. He was now engaged.

CHAPTER 15
HIGH EXPECTATIONS

A few years later Liam O'Brien would say to me: 'We should never have played that game on that pitch'.

I told him that we would have won that game on any pitch or surface, such was the mood of the squad at the time.

I accept that it was hard to explain Setanta's failure to show up on the day.

They seemed to have no fight in them and that surprised me.

They were just very poor. Maybe it was the pressure.

It was a good feeling. They weren't at their best but the thought of us winning gave lads like Philly a bit more incentive.

Setanta were decent guys and didn't cheat that day. They could easily have thrown in two or three bangers from their first team and won it but they didn't.

And it was through our league win, coming as it did after a less than impressive season in 2008, that the team picked up the Fingal sports stars of the month for November.

At the beginning of they year, Sean Madigan as our captain, represented the club at the Fingal Independent Sports Star of the Year awards banquet. Sporting Fingal would pick up the overall award for their FAI Cup win but it was nonetheless a nice feeling to be nominated in good company like that.

There was also the club's dinner dance to look forward to and strangely enough, no one within the club could remember the last time we held one.

In fact no one in the club could remember the last time the club had such success in terms of winning both the championship in football and the league in hurling within weeks of each other.

Amazingly this was the first and second entry into the record books for the Wild Geese which had been in existence for well over a century.

The dinner dance was the first occasion most of the lads were together since the day of the league final. The Coolquay Lodge in The Ward was the venue and it was strange seeing all the players and their partners dressed up to the nines. We get on extremely well as a group but few socialised together, other than the odd post match drink or a special occasion. I was surprised to discover that it was the first county medal most of the lads had won.

Having got a taste for success, we were already looking ahead to the New Year. Good news came through from the juvenile front when Dara O'Brien made the cut for the Dublin team. That's serious progress for a club like ours.

Dara's development was as much down to the hard work of Sean who would have coached the likes of Dara, Sean Dunphy and Mattie King all the way up from the under-10s.

Though a solid defender who never gets caught out of position, he played with the wrong hurling grip.

So 'Flats' told Dara if he was going to make it he would have to switch his grip. He worked hard, was relentless and successfully changed his grip.

Sean told the Dublin selectors that Dara had changed his grip and they had another look at him. This certainly gave all the lads on the squad a lift ahead of the new season. I brought with me a copy of the fixture list for the coming season which had just been distributed by the County Board. Some of the lads' girlfriends were not impressed that we were talking shop but what else were we to talk about. Hurling was our bond!

We were going to be in Division 7 again but this time legitimately and we were excited about it. Shane and Philly were like kids going through the list of opponents; 'eight we never faced before' says Philly. 'Like who?' says Shane. Philly started to name them, 'Skerries, St. Sylvesters, Erin's isle ...'.

Shane jokingly replied:'Ah no bother, we'll handle them'. It was a bit daunting as we didn't really know what to expect.

We enjoyed the evening, the first of many, we hoped.

Dublin footballer Eamon Fennell, who was stuck in a bit of a transfer saga between O'Tooles and St Vincents, was on hand to present the medals.

And at the end of the night, the younger contingent headed to 'Velvet' a local nightclub, while the 'elder lemons' went home.

We had other reasons to be upbeat. Tom Kennedy, an experienced hurler, was transferring to us from Faughs hurling club, while both Shane and Mattie, who was appointed as team captain, had been selected for the initial inter-county Fingal hurling trials.

The Fingal hurling team was at the time a new concept, and was made up of players picked from clubs within one of the four Dublin county council boundaries.

The thinking behind it was simple and honest … to further develop hurling in the region. The idea doesn't sit too well with true blue fans who recall the 2002 strategic review committees suggestions of splitting Dublin in two.

Not helping either was the reluctance of some of the 13 feeder clubs to embrace it. They saw it as taking away players at crucial times of the season.

Fingal had been entered into the Dublin Senior Championship along with a series of other regional teams.

The idea was to give players from less established clubs the chance to play senior hurling but eventually the regional teams fell by the wayside because after three years they were deemed unsuccessful.

It was felt by some members of the management team that the Dublin county board and members of the board did not work hard enough to keep it. Even up to the 2011 season, things were still far from rosy with one former manager going so far as to describe himself as a 'patsy' in the local paper after Fingal had failed to fulfil a league fixture against Roscommon due to lack of numbers.

There was work behind the scenes with Fingal agreeing not to enter a team in the Nicky Rackard in the 2012 championship to allow players to play championship hurling for the clubs during the summer months.

It certainly seemed to ease tensions and speaking personally I had been an advocate of the project from the start.

Anyway, it was easy enough to figure who we were going to send to the trials to be held up at the St Brigid's GAA grounds in January. After some chat we nominated Mattie, Shane, Collie and David Rennie.

The former two were certainly up for it. Dave declined as did Collie who despite being a terrific athlete just felt he wasn't good enough for it.

Though he and Dave may have lacked many of the fundamentals of the game they had enough talent to warrant a trial.

I felt they would benefit from the higher level of training and so would we – nothing selfish in that!

On a dreary cold January Sunday morning, I went over with Mattie and Shane for the initial trial. The lads did okay. I felt they were a bit intimidated as they were from the weakest club of the 13 in Fingal and were a bit conscious of that. Mattie and Shane did not know any of the other players.

After the training, they went indoors for a brief chat. Shane was first out, ready for home. 'Jesus you're out fast! Where's Mattie?' I asked.

'In talking to some of the selectors,' he replied. Ed went with them to the next session in Tallaght. After that, the lads were on their own – we had done our bit. When they announced the Fingal inter-county panel, Mattie was on it, Shane was not. I was surprised as I thought both would be on the fringes. Shane is definitely a more complete hurler but he lacks Mattie's confidence.

When we got news that Mattie had been picked we were thrilled for him while it was a great honour for a small club like ours.

I called Mattie to congratulate him, 'so Mattie what you do you think? Surprised?'

You could hear the happiness in his voice. 'Its crazy to think I only started hurling eighteen months ago and now I am playing with an inter-county team'.

I told him it was a great honour for the club as well as himself and wondered if he would get a GPA grant? He didn't know.

A bunch of us went down to see his first game against Louth in the Kehoe Cup, played in Swords.

It was late January and we were the only spectators at the game.

This year, they got the chance to play in front of a sizeable attendance in Tullamore after reaching the Division 3A final.

Monaghan controversially handed Fingal a walkover following a dispute with the county board to hold football games in the week leading up to the game.

The then manager Mattie Lennon resigned in protest at what he called a lack of respect for his team. It deprived the Fingal players of the chance to play in the dress rehearsal to the Dublin-Galway league relegation play-off.

Back in 2010, Fingal was still very much in the development process and on that day, Mattie did not get a run out but that was his first outing with Fingal.

We could now highlight our promising younger hurlers who could go for a Dublin team and failing that, could try out for Fingal.

Mattie did not get any starts with Fingal but he was introduced as a substitute regularly after that. He managed to score in a few games. All the lads monitored his progress and it became a topic of conversation amongst us.

He came back a much slicker performer to us and his ability to turn a game on its head for Wild Geese was proof of that.

Mattie was always of a very good mindset and I think he learned an awful lot when he was training with them.

That's why I encourage lads to go to Fingal and the Dublin development squads. I want people to know about the Wild Geese. I want us to have a profile and for people to come into the area and for people to want to join our club.

We have a lot of players in the area that play hurling with Finians and Erins Isle and Fingallians.

They were playing before we started up but my hope is that when they are near retirement they might transfer to us. We might be junior F but we are fairly successful and have good penetration rates.

After our success the previous year, I genuinely thought that it would be 'onwards and upwards for 2010'.

I was shocked that the initial numbers for training were so poor. Many of the lads just evaporated, they were not prepared to put in the commitment and training required for a higher level of hurling. They had just won an unexpected county medal and many felt it was a good time to drop out.

Crucially, Collie was going to be unavailable for selection for the season. He got a six month break from work on condition that he would return to his company's new branch in Abu Dhabi if they got busy. His girlfriend Orlaith and he ventured east, taking in many countries on his way to Australia. The day they arrived in Sydney, he got the call from work and had to leave almost immediately. They did six months in the middle-east before spending the remainder of the year in the US and then came home.

A big loss for us too was David Reilly. He had to quit all sports as he was diagnosed with Long QT syndrome which in his case is caused mainly by exercising and adrenaline. He collapsed one day in work that's how he discovered it.

In a weird way it turned out to be a bit of luck as the first sign can be sometimes cardiac arrest. When I heard his news I was shocked; this is the sort of thing that happens to others not to our teammates. I must admit to being a bit relieved too that he did not collapse or get a heart-attack while playing hurling with us. David is a quiet, unassuming lad who got on with everyone. While handy at hurling, he had serious potential as a footballer. It must have been very tough to have to cease all sports at his age.

As a further blow to us, a lot of the fringe dual players just stopped coming. When we contacted them, the gist was 'we cannot serve two masters' and they chose football.

I could understand why but we had never demanded 100 per cent commitment as a requirement to being part of the unit. We knew hurling would play second fiddle to Gaelic football or in some cases soccer.

The reality is hurling needs more skills practice to master than football but the country is awash with footballers.

Philly is presented with his league medal by Eamon Fennell in January 2010.

Daire O'Brien was the first of our juveniles to make the breakthrough to the county team in 2010.

The arrival of Tom Kennedy, 'a Laurent Blanc-type figure', from Faughs hurling club was a big boost.

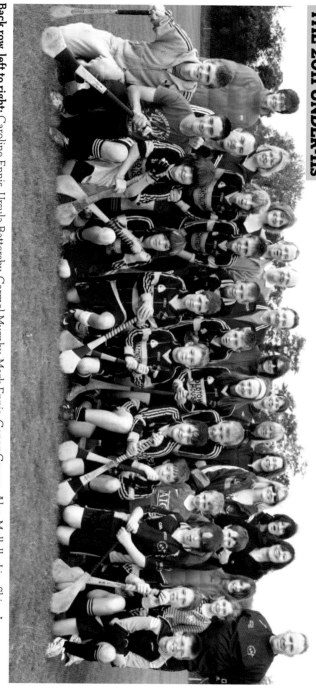

LEAGUE WINNERS: THE 2011 UNDER-11s

Back row, left to right: Caroline Ennis, Ursula Battersby, Carmel Murphy, Mark Ennis, Conor Craven, Alan Mullally, Lisa Shier, Irene O'Brien, Jane Sweetman, Orla Cahalane, Michelle Craven, Breda Kinsella, Adrienne Newman and Sean Flatley. **Middle row:** Ed Sweetman, Liam Shier, Ben O'Brien, Scott Ennis, Michael Battersby, Niamh Sweetman, Patrick Jordan, Callum Creaven, Tony Newman, Heather Newman and Niamh Cahalane. **Front row:** Nathan Monks, Dara O'Brien, Adam Mullally, Aaron Kinsella, Odhran Murphy, Cian Cahalane, Jack O'Brien, Craig Creaven, Conor Newman, Ciara Flatley and Niall Sweetman.

ABOVE: We win 2-8 to 0-6 but Collie's comeback lasts only five minutes.
BELOW: Jordan, Collie, Mick and Philly listen to Ed's words before the start of the 2011 Championship.
RIGHT: 'Flats', Ed (hands on head) and the lads are dejected after another one-point defeat rules out any chances of a second league title in three years,

THE 2012 UNDER-13s

Back row, left to right: David Sammon, Conor Newman, Eoin Creaby, Jamie Clarke, Colm Daly, Eoin O'Donnell, James O'Donnell, Aaron Kinsella and Paul Creaby.

Front row: Liam Monks, Matthew Hanlon, Luke Monks, Daniel Sammon and Luke McCaffery.

Back row, left to right: Stephen O'Meara, Cian Fisher, Peter Butler Anderson, Jonathan Rooney, Sean Dunphy, Dara O'Brien, Mathew King, John Rogers, Conor Creaby, Adam White, Joe O'Donnell, James Maxwell and Sean Flatly. **Front row:** Luke Cullen, Jamie Clarke, Daniel Sammon, Simon Barnwell, Eoghan Creaby, Andy Bell, Jordan Hoey, Liam Monks, Josh McDonagh and Danny Callan.

CLOCKWISE FROM MAIN PHOTOGRAPH: 2012 Captain Mark Kealy about to be hooked; my inspiration, my son Michael; Ciaran Smith is escorted off the field by his daughter Caitlin; 2012 newcomers Enniscorthy's Stephen O'Connor and Slim in action against Lucan Sarsfields. We lost that match by a point.

THE 2012 UNDER-9s

The 2012 Under-10 team. **Back row left to right:** David Butler-Anderson, Mark Murray, Ciaran Jordan, Aidan Reid (behind), Sean Murray, Niall Sweetman, Padraic Flatley, Micheal Galvin (behind), Lorcan McMahon, Beibhin Flatley and Mary Madigan. **Front row:** Adam Tiernan-Keegan, Josh Warren, Luke Monks, Ciaran Galvin, Daire Reid, Cathal Galvin, Liam Moran and Kim Murray.

Back row, left to right: Dave Rennie, Mick Kennedy, Aidan Lenehan, Mark McCaffrey, Danny Monks, John Rennie, Eoin Smyth, Philly McCarthy, Paul Kealy, Stephen O Connor, Tom Kennedy and Danny Kelly. **Front row:** Peter Dunphy, Mattie King, Danny Boxwell, Sean Madigan, Nathan McCaffrey, Tom Smyth, Sean Flatley, Oriol Hally-Garcia, Andy Ryan and Jarlath Kingston.

Paul Kealy watches on as his Wild Geese teammates battle for possession.

To counter those losses Danny Boxell and David 'Beaver' (We never were able to establish where he got the nickname) Dowd from Garristown came. Although neither had ever played before we could see from an early stage they had it in them.

Tom Kennedy's transfer also came through and he certainly ticked all the boxes for us.

An electrician originally from Whitehall, he had hurled all his adult life for Faugh's, who are still Dublin's most successful hurling club.

He and his young family had recently moved to Ballyboughal and as acquaintance of Sean Madigan's, he was persuaded to move to the club.

He was in great shape for a man in his early forties. He cut a Laurent Blanc-type figure and possessed great vision and intelligence on and off the field.

The years of hurling were evident with the precision of his passing at a time when many of our lads were still sending 'haymakers' up the field blindly.

Most of all Tom was a cool customer and his addition certainly gave us a new dimension.

At this stage, we decided to increase the intensity of the training but the initial numbers were so frustratingly low there was little point.

It was particularly hard to take for someone like Sean Madigan, an inspirational figure for us.

Now approaching 40, the injuries were starting to creep up on him and you wouldn't have blamed him if he wanted to take a step back.

He fully embraced the dream and it gave him great satisfaction to see that there were lads from the Wild Geese club who were now making the Dublin development squads.

And as he put it himself: 'If someone had said that to you maybe four or five years ago they would have laughed at you'.

The lack of numbers was something that he found very frustrating.

There were some days when you felt you didn't want to go but if you make that commitment, then you were letting down the rest of your team.

As he recalled later on, there were some players carrying injuries who would attend training and then there were those who just didn't bother turning up.

Work was also beginning to take its toll with few in the declining economic climate prepared to take time off or switch shifts for games that clashed with work.

The County board did its best to stick to the master fixture list but clubs with inter-county players were at times making this hard with one prominent club forcing two Fingal clubs to move fixtures because it hadn't the numbers to field a team.

You couldn't blame players for being vexed when after switching shifts to play a game, they were still having to deal with this kind of carry on.

At the lower end of the leagues there probably wasn't as big an incentive to turn up, as players were having to put work before play.

In Ciaran's case, his wife Martina went back working nights as an A&E nurse in Beaumont hospital. He had three young girls under five, and with a demanding job with various shift work patterns, spare time was a commodity he had little of.

He made it clear he wanted to continue to be part of the unit but could not make the same commitment. You had to make allowances for that. If we had 10 turning up for a session that was a good turnout. The poor numbers had a sort of domino effect. We did not fall out with the absentees, we couldn't as we needed them for the games. I think we realised that this was going to be our first really tough year. It looked like Ed was right about promotion being a poisoned chalice. Many felt they had reached their hurling zenith and the repercussions were felt by the rest of us.

For those who remained, it was still a thrill to play hurling. We were a journey, not a destination. The season also saw Dicey retire from hurling and the management to concentrate solely on football.

CHAPTER 16

TRIUMPH OF FAILURE

Our first game of the season was in the cup against Na Flanna's second team.

We were familiar with their third team and had beaten them a few times, so this was a different proposition. The fixture clashed with a load of football cup games, so we had only the bare minimum of players.

It was the first time we had played with a live scoreboard. The only problem was with our reading of it! We were never at the races losing 2-14 to 2-5. Mattie was a revelation, arguably the best player on the field, he scored 2-4 from play.

On the way home Peter and I talked about the remarkable change in Mattie's hurling in such a short time. Training twice a week and for longer periods with 20 others of a similar standard was paying off after just five weeks.

For our first league game of the season at the end of March, Mattie was away on Fingal duty. It was the worst possible start, another lethargic display, beaten 2-11 to 0-7.

Tommy Kehoe was the ref and as I was walking off, he commented: 'You were rusty there, Aidan'.

'You are being kind, Tommy' I said.

Last year Whitehall couldn't beat us now they had just brushed us a side.

One positive we could take from the game was a point Philly scored from a sideline cut. He and Tom Kennedy had started practicing it in training and they had a competition going. Now he had opened his account. There was only 12 points scored from sideline pucks in the 2010 senior hurling Championship, thus underlining Philly's achievement.

He deserved it as he was still out of work and was now officially 'on the dole and depressed'.

Even the interviews had dried up and he's wasn't the type of lad that could just lie in bed all day.

We had Mattie back for our second league game, away to Skerries Harps. At the back of my mind there was always the impression they looked down on us. We had played them once in a challenge which they won with ease but we were never asked for a rematch after that, even though I had sought it.

On the other hand I found it surprising to find a town with their population and size with only one hurling team in the lower ranks.

They lost two of their better juvenile players to another club on the understanding they would come back when they came of age as part of a gentleman's agreement.

They never sought to use that as an excuse and their work at under-age saw call ups to both the panels of the North Dublin Colleges squads and Fingal squads in 2012.

I suppose we were looked upon as cannon fodder. So this for me was a big test. It was a warm April Sunday afternoon and I expected us to have a full team out. A beaming Paul Kealy was first to arrive. He had just landed some part-time work with MSD Swords. Needless to say when he told the lads that he was packing 'the pill' there where many smart comments from the less mature fraction within the dressing room.

We started well, matching them in every area of the field. Beaver was on fire that day winning lots of ball and getting fouled continuously as he went towards goal. Dave Rennie duly obliged by putting the frees over the bar. They got a lucky goal just before the half-time break to keep them in at 0-7 to 1-3. Again the second half was a re-run of the first in many ways but their greater experience began to tell as they nudged ahead for the first time with eight minutes to go. Skerries finished in emphatic fashion, and we had no reply. We ran out of steam – final score 2-10 to 0-9.

While we could walk away with our heads held high it was one that got away and the atmosphere in the dressing-room testified to that. They were the Goliath and on this occasion David's sling had failed him.

It didn't get better in our next league game when we lost to Parnell's 1-13 to 0-9.

They were a young, fit team with lots of natural hurling ability and it was like trying to keep up with the Red Arrows.

We were coming up against exceptionally strong teams and performing well but obviously lacked the talent to defeat them. The expectations we had were well and truly gone after the Parnell's defeat. The best we could hope for was to nick a win or two and then hope that that would be sufficient to stay up.

Myself, Peter and Ed agreed that it was important we keep things together. There would be no panic and no talk of abandoning ship.

Certainly we recognised that a lot of the guys had not been playing for that long and hurling was a game that required a lot of skill.

We knew at the same time that while we had overshot the runway of success, our skill levels had not risen in tandem.

Things didn't improve in the next game against St Oliver Plunketts/Eoghan Ruadh when we were annihilated. Once again the decision to run cup matches in the football was to leave our squad threadbare. Frustrations were starting to come to the surface with both Shane and Beaver picking up red cards in that game.

We were out of our depth at this stage.

'There is no joy in this, the sooner we get relegated the better,' said 'Flats', summing up precisely how we all felt coming off the field. It didn't help that our lack of discipline let us down.

It was hard enough to compete at this level with 15. Having only 13 meant we had shot ourselves in the foot.

Little by little the team was losing heart which meant it was more important than ever to keep talking positive to them. It put our managerial skills to the test.

The next day I got a text from Philly:'I'm not sure if I'll be able to continue to play' it read while he also alluded to being 'broken up playing hurling'. It was a bolt from the blue. Philly's luck had turned in the previous few weeks. He was now working in a pet-shop and was thrilled to be earning again.

I texted him back immediately telling him I would call into him on the way home from work. Philly had been back to himself of late so as I entered the shop where he worked, I genuinely didn't know what to expect.

He met me at the door wearing his Wild Geese hurling hoodie. This was a good sign I thought.

Anyway he ushered me upstairs to an office where I was met by the stale smell of tobacco smoke even though the window was open for ventilation.

He sat in behind an office desk and produced a packet of cigarettes. He offered me one.

'Will I need it?' I asked as I sat down opposite him.

'Look I am pissed off about this but I see no way around it', he said.

I was at a loss as to what he meant. 'What are you on about, Philly', I asked again.

Philly had played cup football the evening before and missed our annihilation. And as Plunkett's were dishing out a heavy defeat, it looked as if Margaret's were conspiring against us too.

Margarets were managed by Paul Clarke, who needed no introduction if you were from the capital.

Having captained Dublin to All Ireland minor success in the GAA's centenary year, he was part of the famous '91 saga involving Dublin and Meath.

Clarkie reached his promised land four years later when Dublin captured the Sam against Tyrone and later became part of the Dublin management team under Paul Caffrey.

A much respected coach, he took the reins at St Margarets who were aiming to gain promotion to Division Two.

Philly chipped in: 'Clarkie had a meeting of all the St. Margaret's intermediate footballers after last night's game. He told us he didn't want his players getting broken up playing other sports'.

I laughed and nearly choked on the tobacco smoke. He was saying that it would not be good for their GAA development to play other sports.'

I wasn't sure if I was hearing right. Surely Clarkie was aware that there was more than one code in the GAA. Truthfully though, this was not as bad as I had been expecting, especially as Philly was not entirely sold on the idea.

He was really important to us, a jolly lad, inspirational, and was a vital cog in the wheel on and off the field. He probably has the strongest personality on the panel and is immensely popular.

It was my turn now to make my case and I knew I had to keep him with us one way or another. 'Philly, you and I both know that hurling is a much safer game to play. When you're playing football, you use your body continuously, be it to win the ball, block down, tackles etc. In hurling, particularly in your case, you have 38 inches of ash between you and the ball, so you are a lot less likely to get injured in the long run.

'If you want to stay away from hurling training for a bit and stop playing friendlies, no problem. Look, keep your head down, say nothing to Clarkie and it will blow over but please stick with us,' I pleaded.

He leaned back and pulled on the fag. 'Alright so,' he said, matter of factly. He liked the idea of taking a back seat for a bit, thus avoiding any confrontation with the football management. In time, as I predicted, it blew over. I said nothing to anyone until Philly was well and truly back on board. Months later in a conversation with his St. Margarets clubmate Sean Madigan about it, he said: 'Look if the football management could see past their noses, they'd realise that with the rotation system in Dublin, playing hurling keeps their players away from soccer and that's the sport they are losing most players to.'

To hear that from a clubmate was important and it was a brave and committed decision Philly had made in sticking with us.

With the Philly issue resolved or parked for the time being, we could turn our attentions to the first round of the championship in what was our first competitive game of the season.

It proved a morale booster of sorts as we went on to defeat an understrength St Peregrines team. For our next fixture, we received a walkover against St Joseph's/O'Connell Boys as they were unable to field a team.

We had now qualified for the Junior E championship quarter-finals after two fixtures because the first four of the six teams group qualify and we had enough points already.

Our third game in the group against old rivals Setanta saw us return to the scene of our league final win in Ballymun.

In the dressing-rooms beforehand, I couldn't put my finger on why but the mood was not right. Mattie is a decent leader on the field but not an inspiring talker and so I asked the injured Sean Madigan to take the reins for the pre-match talk.

He opened up the Evening Herald, showed the lads that we were sitting on top of the group and explained that we needed to win to maintain that. As he spoke I looked around and saw that some of the lads seemed very laid back that evening.

From the throw-in, we looked a pale shadow of the team that had beaten Setanta twice in seven days the previous November.

Setanta were back to themselves and even though Mattie had an off day, I was taken off midway through the second half.

I had no qualms about it but as Peter sought to remedy one situation, another situation was unfolding on the field.

Beaver had picked up a yellow card early on and having subsequently mouthed off at the ref was treading a very thin line.

In situations like these, referees will occasionally advise the line to replace a man to avoid sending a man off. This ref signalled to Peter that it might be a wise decision to take Beaver off rather than lose a player to a second yellow.

Peter took note and duly called Beaver to the line and while we managed to keep our full allotment of players, Beaver didn't quite see it that way.

Immediately he threw down his helmet while Peter talked to him on the ills of talking back to a referee.

This seemed to incite Beaver even more with verbals ensuing between the two.

I tried to reason with Beaver stressing 'that no amount of talking to a ref would make him change his decision even if he thought it was the wrong decision. The best thing to do was to let the hurl do the talking.'

The three of us stood there for the last few minutes in an uneasy truce and that was the end of that drama. As we reflected on another poor team display, with just one score from play, I couldn't understand what had gone so wrong lately.

We were beginning to play like lads that had never played together before. The run of defeats had shattered our self-belief and to make matters worse Beaver didn't turn up for training or our next championship game against Civil Service on the following Sunday.

In all fairness things get said in the heat of the match that people do not mean but on this occasion it was very tame, 'hand bag' stuff. I tried calling the lad but he never answered.

I asked Peter was there anything more said to him on the sideline other then what I heard; he said there was not.

We have enough keen lads but he was a loss, as he had shown potential to be a good forward and we would never see him again.

Our game with Civil Service was another write off as we lost 3-6 to 1-3.

We now realised that it was going to be a long hard summer on the hurling field.

One of the big achievements was that we managed to keep the team together and tried to remain as upbeat as possible.

We were on a journey to relegation – that we knew, so we figured these encounters could and should improve us, as we were quite naive when it came to hurling. When table-topping Erin's Isle came to Oldtown for our league game, I had the lads well briefed.

The plan was to contain them, keep the score respectable. At half time they where 1-3 to 0-4 up.

I reiterated my original stance and Shane's belief at half-time that 'these lads weren't good and that we could take them' proved to be an overstatement to say the least.

Erin's Isle won the second-half 2-11 to no score but there was some respite when Philly returned full-time for our next game (St Margarets had just exited the intermediate championship).

He was no sooner back in a friendly against Termonfeckin when he received a belt of a hurl on the head.

The frustrating thing for us was that he had a helmet but just refused to wear it.

The cut just above the eyebrow was bad enough, bleeding heavily and definitively required stitches.

I wondered what Clarkie would say if he saw him now.

Thankfully Ciaran Smith was on hand to administer some modern glue that has replaced stitches today. A few days later, you could hardly see the cut. Philly didn't finish that game as a precaution and he wore a beanie hat at football training the next two nights to hide the scars. The cut was not noticed although I'm sure there were a few comments made about the beanie hat!

When I heard we had drawn Skerries away in the championship quarter final, I didn't know whether to laugh or cry. They were raging favourites, the form team and had demolished most of their opposition. How do you prepare for a bout, you know you have no hope in?

We were in a much weaker state then when we faced up to them in the league. On the morning of the game, as I drove to Skerries, I got four texts, all last minute withdrawals.

I am glad Peter was with me to witness it, otherwise you may have thought I had made it up. I suppose everyone knew what was in store, our two best lads were missing. Shane by now had committed to playing soccer (he would go on to win player of the year at Swords Celtic in 2011) while Mattie was injured from playing football with Ravens.

Added to that John Rennie was on holidays and Philly was at a christening. Ed, Sean Madigan and Floody where also injured from playing football. We were seriously tight but started anyway with 14. We had always prided ourselves on putting out a team regardless of the circumstances and we weren't going to stop now.

With all these late withdrawals we were facing something we had met before.

It was a shambles. Nothing in the book prepares you for this.

But we had gone too far to throw in the towel. Dave Rennie, who had slept it out, came along just before half-time, so at least we had the regulation numbers required.

To our credit, we matched them in first-quarter but that was as good as it got.

The next fifteen minutes saw Skerries hit us for two goals.

to leave the half-time score at 2-5 to 0-2. During the break Ed lectured us about 'standing up for ourselves and about having pride in the jersey.'

He might as well have been talking to a bunch of Christians about to be led out into the coliseum to face hungry lions for all the good it did but at least he tried. No amount of fire and brimstone could have worked. No miracles that day.

We kept giving the ball away and were constantly under pressure in all areas of the field. In defeat, at what stage do you give up? That day we subconsciously gave up before the game even commenced. We lost 3-19 to 0- 4 which was a real humiliation.

Ed gathered us together at the end of the game.

Our last league game of the season was against our old nemesis Setanta. This was the sixth time we had played them competitively in two years. Familiarity breeds contempt? 'Not them again,' was the reply Liam O'Brien got from his charges when he told them of the fixture.

The week before the game Mark Kealy told us he had secured full time employment as a gravedigger in Dardistown cemetery and Floody had started work at the check out in IKEA. His plan was to get in and work his way into the plumbing section, his area of expertise. This was the first time we had seen them since they started the new careers.

There was lots of light-hearted slagging taking place, especially directed at Mark but you could see he was thrilled. Almost two years had past since he had worked on a full-time basis. While Floody had been in and out of plumbing jobs, the guarantee of weekly income was a relief to him. These two successes were against the national trend because unemployment was still rising but not at the same rate. It now stood at 13.5 per cent. Maybe the fact that we were now relegated seemed to take some pressure off us at this stage.

Setanta were safely sitting in mid-table and had nothing to play for only pride. I was particularly happy with my own performance in the first-half after scoring three points from play. Some days you're just in the right place at the right time.

I was being marked by Liam O'Brien and I made it my business not to acquaint myself with the lad who was marking me and certainly never got involved in chit-chat.

It's definitely harder to play on a lad you know and especially someone you had a lot of time for. So after I scored the first point, Liam remarked; 'there's life in the old dog yet'. I couldn't help but smile.

Overall it was a good-humoured game with only one or two flash points. Nonetheless after two opponents had squared up to each other, referee Aidan Fitzsimons managed to take the heat out of the moment.

'Come on now lads, you are starting to sound like footballers. Play hurling and get on with it,' he commented for all our amusement.

The game ended in a draw 0-13 to 1-10, a good result for us given how things had been with us for a while.

There was triumph in us sticking together and not letting the series of defeats knock us over and while we were relegated, we had survived and did not fold. We kept on telling ourselves that we were new to this and it would get better.

The camaraderie had grown amongst us in the face of adversity. Adult hurling in the area had survived its first major setback.

CHAPTER 17
COMEBACK SEASON

When the fixtures for the new season were released by the county board, I was disappointed to find us buried in division nine of the hurling league and Junior F of the hurling championship. There was an F in hurling!

Since we had started the team in 2008, 12 new teams had taken up the challenge. Most were third teams from big clubs. One was St. Patrick's of Donabate. They had followed our developments closely and we had advised them and played a few challenges against them before they took the plunge in 2010.We had not expected to find ourselves in the lowest division of hurling in Dublin.

A bureaucratic mistake by the county board had seen us moved down two league divisions to division nine and not division eight as it should have been. This demotion was without any notification and subsequently they had shifted us from Junior E championship to Junior F as well.

I was insulted. Try explaining to a lad down the country that you play Junior F and he will think you're absolute rubbish and wonder can you hit a ball. I was confident I could get this wrong corrected but first I wanted to see what the lads thought.

Our first training session of the year was due, so we arranged to meet 20 minutes early to discuss the issue. We had a good turnout and began an open discussion on the matter. Mark said it might be what we needed to restore our confidence after a bruising 2010 campaign.

I didn't agree. 'Mark, division 9 could be harder to win than division 8. There is a conveyor belt of young teams coming through from some of the bigger clubs. Look at Castleknock for example,' I continued. 'They were only founded in 1998, now they have a Junior A hurling team, they started a second team last year and will have a third team for Junior F this year. They were the first ever Dublin club to win Feile Na Gael hurling A in 2005, now those kids are coming of age and they have plenty of hurling'. Sean cut me off: 'Sure you might as well meet them in Junior F as well as in Junior E'.

'Fair enough, I suppose all I am saying is to win Junior F, won't be as easy as you might think'.

Mattie was asked what he thought. 'I suppose given the year we just had, it might be better to stay where we are'. That input was decisive. He was after all, our inter-county player.

'Shane you're our captain this year, what do you think?' Ed asked. 'I'm not bothered'.

'All right then, will we leave it as it is ?' I asked everyone.

'Yes' was the general consensus from all those present. Junior F it was to be.

The struggle to have intensive training sessions continued because of the poor numbers. We hadn't got any new recruits but Tom Smyth committed to hurling after a break, which was a big boost. The panel was now a small group of dedicated hurlers, most of whom had been there since the beginning. A strong sense of friendship had developed among the group over the years and I felt if we could use this, we could repeat the success of 2009. Unfortunately Gooch quit for good this time. He is an apprentice mechanic and soccer is his first love and then Gaelic football.

'I genuinely do not have the time to hurl as well,' he told me.

He was a loss but had become unreliable for games. On the jobs front, Ed had worries, Diageo, the firm he works for as an electrician had just announced that they were cutting the work force. No more information was forthcoming from the firm but a dark cloud loomed. The club had managed to do its bit by getting our corner-back Danny Kelly on a three day FAS scheme as a groundkeeper. It had been a few years since Danny had steady work and this was a welcome boost for him and his young family. Danny is football-mad but embraced the hurling, gave it a go and unlike other lads who could not master it at first, stuck with it. While he did not get much play time in the beginning, he does now. He persevered.

His son Daniel accompanies him to many of the home matches. He glides around the place with a hurl in his hand most times I see him. Progress comes in many guises.

For Shane the final stages of his carpentry apprenticeship was proving very difficult, he had done his time in college but getting the six months experience needed was proving next to impossible, at least in one swoop. A few weeks work here or there was all he could get and no qualified carpenter was willing to sponsor him. Most of his mates were now unemployed. Some had gone to Australia but everyone was advising him to stick with it. 'Work on your qualifications and then head down under if you want'.

The work had completely dried up for Tom Kennedy and he too was worried about the future. What are the options open to an unemployed man in his early forties with a young family?

Later in February, Mattie told us he had quit the Fingal panel, explaining that he needed to study in the evenings for accountancy exams.

Playing for the Fingal team took a lot of effort and dedication and he had gone back training with them at the start of 2011 but had also started college at night.

He knew pretty early that he could not be fully committed so one had to go. Unfortunately hurling does not put bread on the table so he had to stop playing. There is also the case that he probably did not have the confidence and belief in himself that he could become a starting player. Also he had missed a lot of football when he played for Fingal.

The upside of that was we would see more of him and he would be available for all league games. And while there was good news with Mattie playing for us full-time, we were to lose the services of Larry McDermott, the economic environment of the time meant that the Dublin Country board needed a contribution from us to keep him and the funds just weren't there.

It was a sad parting, especially as the latest nursery batch of hurlers, with whom he had spent many hours, graduated to an U7 team. The reins were now taken by Ballyboughal man, Aidan Reid, a Chief Superintendent in the Garda Siochana.

On the adult front we learned very quickly that all the teams in Division 9 had a similar ability to us but we got off to a good start, two wins and two draws. The latter were games I felt we had left behind. Still four games in a row unbeaten was new territory for us. We were fired up for the start of the Junior F hurling championship.

First up was Good Counsel, a team from the south inner city. We won 2-8 to 0-6; Mattie was outstanding, scoring 1-4 from play. Collie's hurling comeback after 18 months break only lasted a few minutes; he pulled a hamstring within five minutes of coming on. Afterwards I was chatting to himself and Orlaith, his partner. I asked him what he thought of our performance, given he had not seen us play in 2010 and had avoided the trench warfare of Division 7.

I knew I'd get an honest insight. 'You're very heavily reliant on Mattie' was his answer. That was not the answer I was hoping for. 'We are,' I replied defensively, 'but sure where would Galway be without Joe Canning or Kilkenny without King Henry?'

It was true, he was our most effective player, and I cannot quibble with that but Collie could not see much real progress in his absence. That frank assessment was a worry. The next Championship game against Naomh Barrog saw us back to our old ways. Even Mattie could not pull this one out of the fire. It did not help that we were tight on numbers. Philly could not make it he 'he had to wait for a delivery of exotic fish'. I never got that excuse before.

Sean Flatley was outstanding in goals. Thanks to him the scoreline was kept to respectable levels.

Great news came through that Sean Dunphy had got the call to the U14 Dublin development squad. Daire was still with the U15s and prospering, so having a second breakthrough so soon was a boost. He got word at the Feile na nGael. The County board had suggested we host it and we were keen but you need two pitches. So when some brave soul further suggested Fingal Ravens give us use of their grounds, many eye brows were raised. Ravens were all on for it and while our U-14 team finished bottom out of the five teams, the day was an amazing success and highlighted the reconciling effect the hurling had in the area.

Interestingly St. Brigids had a team involved and those kids were taken away for a break in the middle of the Feile to Roganstown leisure club and brought into the swimming pool.

It was paid for the by the club. They all had bowls of pasta for lunch and some had massages. It was something that certainly amazed Sean McNulty our chairman.

The way he saw it you either had the hurling ability or not. If you haven't got a certain amount of ability, all the pasta in the world and all the rubbing won't make a different. Brigid's went on to win their Feile grade. I wondered if it was within us given our Jekyll and Hyde performances.

When we were good we were very good as was the case when we trounced St.Oliver Plunkets/Eoghan Rua. Thunder and lightning greeted us as we left the dressing-rooms. Right from the off we meant business. Nathan was unlucky not to score a goal midway through the first-half but the 'keeper managed to parry it, into my path, I got it into my hands, shortened the grip and buried it. I got a second five minutes into the second-half, a hopeful puck from 20 metres, straight into the bottom corner. We won 2-5 to 0-2. Nathan at midfield and Shane at centre-back were brilliant. Were things starting to look up?

A week later we lost two league games in quick succession. The game against Lucan Sarsfields was played on the longest day of the year. The weather was horrible, grey clouds with continuous rain. We led by a point with 25 minutes to go, only to lose by nine. The following Monday we welcomed new rivals St. Pats, Donabate. Our first competitive game against them, we lost 1-10 to 3-6. Two soft goals at crucial times killed us. Two more losses in the championship, one a heavy one away to St. Marks, Tallaght and another against St.Joseph's/O'Connell Boys, meant we faced a must win game against Parnells. The latter defeat was particularly hard to take, as we led by ten points at half-time, some appalling refereeing and poor finishing cost us dearly.

The Parnells 1-13 to 1-3 win was for me our greatest championship result yet. It was a must-win game. I scored the goal but Mattie made it, he took possession mid-way, soloed in and drew my marker out of position. He then passed it with deadly accuracy and all I had to do was sidestep their goalkeeper, tap it into the empty net. It was one of the few days we have had since the beginning where everything went perfectly. If I had my time over again, those 60 minutes would stay unchanged. For me it was proof that we could become a force again.

The quarter-final of the championship saw us pitted against Lucan Sarsfields away. They had turned us over in a league game on 21st June. It was a hard draw and then the winner would have the pleasure of St. Marks in the semi-final. That would be next to impossible to win but a semi-final berth would represent progress. This was the third time in a row we had got to the championship quarter-finals but the first that I believed we had a real chance of winning.

We had the lads well primed and ready for the occasion. It was a cold blustery day in September. We won the toss and Shane opted to play with the wind. That's always been our policy, take what ever advantage you can when it's available. The wind may die down for the second-half.

As it turned out, it did not and the elements played a major part in the game. From the off it was a physical game as a phenomenal amount of hurls where broken as the clash of the ash intensified. We made the breakthrough midway through the first-half when Chris Keane wriggled free in the right hand corner, hand-passed to the unmarked John Rennie who made no mistake.

That goal lifted us and for the next 10 minutes we ran the show. Shane Byrne made a great high catch, from the resulting Lucan Sarsfields puck out; he spotted Dave Rennie on the wing and delivered. Rennie from a tight angle managed to get his shot in but it dropped short, only for the 'keeper to fumble it. The green flag went up. We were sailing with the aid of the wind. A Tom Kennedy point from a 65' brought us up to half-time. We went in 2-3 to 0-2 ahead. As dominant as we had been in the first-half we had not managed to deliver it on the score board. What were the odds of us holding on? There was tension as we listened to Ed and Peter. The plan was to play a short-passing game, thus avoiding the wind. 'Keep possession,' was ringing in our ears as the game recommenced. We started off well with Mattie and Collie combining to score. Mattie followed that up with another individual effort. We were now nine points ahead. Then we gifted them a goal. Sean caught an incoming shot and while trying to clear it, his effort was blocked with the ball ricocheting into our net. I was afraid heads would drop and then indiscipline began to take root.

Silly hand on the back fouls, then arguing with the referee which only resulted in us giving them more ground, turning into frees from poor angles into certainties that could be scored. Was it nervousness?

Andy Ryan and John Rennie got involved in a heated debate with the referee. The instructions from the line to them were simple; 'lads just shut up and play hurling'. It had no effect. They ignored it. In one case a harmless free from near the Lucan goal was moved 10 metres for dissent. As a consequence they pointed the free with the aid of the breeze. It punctured us. Point by point our lead diminished until Lucan went ahead. We had self-destructed and lost by a point. No one said a word afterwards in the dressing-room.

Only five lads turned up at the following training session. That was as demoralising as the quarter-final defeat but Tom Kennedy had just secured full-time employment with the Dublin Airport Authority and told us that night. That was great news, although the shift-work patterns meant we would definitely see less of him.

By now we had nothing to play for in the league – only pride. I joked with the lads before our last game that a win would secure the final champions league spot. The winner of our encounter would finish fourth in the Division. The first thing Ed noticed, as we warmed up, was the referee was the same one we had against St.Joseph's/O'Connell boys in the championship.

It was a weird game, we were the better team but two early soft goals had them leading from the off. Mattie was in outstanding form, a bit of a one-man show from him. We introduced Ed at half time. In his first altercation he fouled his man, the referee blew up and then Ed got his chance to tell him exactly what he thought of him. He did not hold back and got a straight red card for it. He winked at me, as he walked to the line.

That incident seems to wake us up and we managed to do enough to win the game. At the end I joked with Ed: 'You can't retire now, you cannot go out like that'. He did not answer but it was plain see he was happy.

We all congratulated Mattie on his great performance. He had scored 13 of our 15 points, with nine from frees. It was a decent end to the season. Every one was upbeat, the lads were trying to plan a hurling weekend away. I perhaps naively could never have predicted the advancing storm that would rock the foundations we had laid.

CHAPTER 18

• • • • • • • • • • • • • • • •
PARISH RULE
- OR LACK OF IT
• • • • • • • • • • • • • • • • • • •

Before we get to the transfer that knocked us back on our seats, allow me to digress a little bit.

Coming from rural Ireland, it was engrained in you that you played with the team in the parish, either where you lived or where you were from. No ifs, buts or maybes.

Probably because they are so rare in the GAA, transfers have often been controversial and there has been a fair amount of transfer sagas. The great Christy Ring was born in Cloyne and hurled with them until the age of 18, then transferred to city side Glen Rovers where he won 13 county titles.

Cloyne still lament his loss and the complete absence of any county senior hurling titles is often attributed to that. They still erected a life-size bronze statue in the village in his honour and claim him as their own but his club successes all came at Glen Rovers. Go into a pub in the village and they will not say a bad word about the legend. Most books about the man glide over this period but Donal Óg Cusack, in his autobiography 'Come what May' touches on it and possibly gives us a truer picture. He tells us that at the time some people broke windows in the Ring family home. He speaks of the 'sadness of Cloyne and also the hope that we should be strong enough, that no great player would ever want to leave again'.

In his book 'The Godfather of Modern Hurling', one of the country's leading hurling writers Enda McEvoy gives us an insight to life before (like Dublin is today) and after the introduction of the parish rule.

The county in question is Kilkenny, the time is 1954 where there was no parish rule. The club scene was dominated by the super clubs like Carrickshock, Mooncoin, Tullaroan and Eire Óg. The county team up until then had won 13 All-Irelands, four minor All-Irelands and one national league.

In his book, McEvoy tells of 'the Rower team that won the 1944 junior championship only to lose seven of their best players to the senior clubs within the space of one year'. And don't forget this was a time when the only locals likely to have a car would have been the priest and the doctor. He continues that 'it took Rower 12 years to get competitive again'.

Responsible for one of the most crucial rule changes in the history of the association was Paddy Buggy who I have been lucky enough to meet on two occasions. Buggy, (a former GAA president), and many others, including those from these so-called super clubs saw the folly of the old system. McEvoy describes it brilliantly: 'A shaft of light split the gloom in 1954.'

On foot of a proposal by Slieverue seconded by Tullaroan, the parish rule was introduced initially on a trial basis before being officially written into law. All changed utterly for the better. Let it be said, there was no suggestion that Buggy, who moved the motion, was acting out of self-interest. Slieverue, Buggy's club ended up losing four first-choice players who lived just the wrong side of the parish boundary.

New clubs popped up and the competitions became much more democratic and most importantly competitive. The game boomed. The county team never looked back and since then have won 21 senior All-Irelands, 16 minor titles and 13 national leagues. Rower amalgamated with Inistioge and eventually won the county title in 1968, lead by Eddie Keher.

But Dublin was different. There is no parish rule here and never has been one. Historically the GAA was weak in the capital; this was the bastion of British power. The foreign games flourished.

Many country people helped found and played with the newly established GAA city clubs but their link was more to do with work than with where they were from or where they resided. Certainly I know many of our junior hurlers today may not be considered local and are not from the parish.

In some cases we have benefitted from the lack of a parish rule but I can give you numerous examples of lads from the parish playing at a higher level with other clubs. The purpose of the rule is to ensure that local teams are made up by locals. Some of the side effects of its absence in Dublin only recently dawned on me. Dublin GAA clubs in contrast to their county cousins have a general lack of basic outdoor spectator facilities that coincides with a lack of spectators at games and lack of atmosphere.

This is partly down to very little identity from the local population with the local team and thus the finger has to be pointed at the absence of a parish rule or a clear boundary between neighbouring clubs.

I believe it's one of the reasons Dublin have failed to capitalise on its enormous advantage of population over the other 31 counties. People go on about the great Dublin support but it doesn't really exist at grassroots level.

There can be little doubt that to introduce a parish rule of sorts would be very difficult to administer in the city and would be very controversial. Today this is not just a Dublin issue but is becoming prevalent in the cities of Cork and Galway as well. Caltra, a tiny GAA club in East Galway, would never have won a club All-Ireland in 2003, if they were a Dublin club. The city's smaller clubs struggle to survive and rarely if ever taste success.

There is a belief in Dublin among players and many coaches that if they play with a small club their career will not progress in the same way as it would at a bigger club. This in turn often leads to a lot of players falling between the two stools with the more powerful 'super clubs' sucking up the most talented from the smaller units.

The end of December and early January in Dublin is the only time transfers are permitted, it's like 'open season' with 152 players in the county requesting transfers in 2012 with many of them key players.

But playing for a smaller club should not be seen as a handicap. The starting 15 of the Cork team that won the All-Ireland senior football championship final in 2010 had eight players all of whom came from clubs that did not play senior club football in the county that year.

Two of them even played at junior level for their club. If you're good enough, it should not make any difference. Do the players from the smaller clubs miss out on the intensity – it doesn't appear so. The GAA ethos is based on the local club.

In fact, the first county teams were actually club teams. So players chopping and changing clubs goes very much against the grain of the organisation. That has not been forgotten in Cork and Conor Counihan did not overlook these eight players just because their club does not play at senior level. That throws the intensity arguments out the window.

The rule continues to draw much debate and controversy with players often left in a limbo.The most recent case involved Eamon Fennell who was involved in a lengthy transfer between his former club O'Toole's and St Vincent's and he is now cleared to play with them.

It was at the time Fennell's contention that not enough was being done to develop football at a club which had been predominately known as one of Dublin's hurling strongholds.

O'Toole's footballers would subsequently gain promotion to Division One at the end of 2011 with a team that included Dublin hurlers, Peadar and Michael Carton.

Their opponents in that promotion final were Fingallians, a club that was to have a major bearing on the shaping of our team the following season. Like O'Toole's in football, Fingallians were a club that sought success in both codes.

Both their football and hurling teams went down a grade in their respective championships and it wouldn't be long before the latter went knocking on Mattie Lambe's door.

CHAPTER 19
TRANSFER SAGA

Being a part of the Fingal panel might have heightened Mattie's ambitions as a player and many in the club felt he might never had left were it not for the exposure he got playing with Fingal.

But at the end of the day we felt he was always one of us and it must be remembered he had never picked up a hurl prior to joining us. To this day, I hadn't the faintest notion that he wanted to leave. A year earlier, before we settled for division 9 and Junior F, we let him have his say and although I felt we were holding him back at times, nothing was said.

Mattie is a quiet person and in his own way, he is cool and hip, the kind of guy teenagers would look up too. He's in no way egotistical, he's a superb and dedicated athlete, who took his sports seriously. I recall coming home from a game once, some of the lads were talking of getting a Chinese and a few pints. They asked Mattie what his post-match meal was going to be. 'Porridge' was his reply. When he spoke the others listened.

Last December he grabbed my attention but for all the wrong reasons. I had not seen or heard from any of the lads for a while. The season was finished a few weeks. Next time we'd be together would be at the annual Christmas party in Oldtown house.

I knew something was up when Mattie's name came flashing up on my phone screen. That was unusual because he never rang me. 'Maybe he can't come to the party,' I hoped.

'Howya Mattie, how's things,' I asked rather apprehensively.

We chatted for a while although I sensed something was on his mind. Eventually he got to the point and then my hurling world, was shattered into smithereens with the four words: 'I want a transfer',

I was dumbfounded.

'Sorry Mattie, what's that you said,' I asked.

He repeated: 'I want a transfer'.

I just froze. There was no place to run or hide and eventually I composed myself. 'Why, what's wrong?'

He replied: 'Nothing, I just want to play at a higher level'.

I responded 'What about the lads and all we have been through together?'

He was brutally honest: 'Look the team has stalled, a lot of the senior lads can't train due to other commitments, which I feel makes it harder for us to progress. I want to prove myself at a higher level, while I still have time'.

'Where are you looking to go to?' I asked. 'Fingallians' he replied. 'Fingallians. Mattie why would want to move from a junior F club, where hurling is the dominant code, to a club that football is considered king but has a junior A hurling team,' I said.

Under Mick Kennedy, Fingallians had won the Junior A Championship in 2010 with future footballing All Star, Paul Flynn, lining out for them the day they defeated St Jude's up in Parnell Park.

Kennedy, a former Dublin minor, had played with Fingallians in the late 1990s and while the club's fortunes in that code would dip somewhat, the arrival of Derry Murphy would see their fortunes rise once more.

Murphy had brought through the likes of Niall Gilligan and Davy Fitzgerald while coaching down in Clare, and was also one of the leading lights with the Fingal hurling management team along with Denis Murphy.

The 2011 season saw them lose their intermediate status after a relegation play-off with Vincents second string but they still had a strong nucleus of players which included the likes of John Matthew Sheridan from St Maurs and Paul Quinn formerly of the O'Dwyers club. Other notables included Peter Daly and Dermot Vaughan who both would make the Nicky Rackard team of the year at different stages in their career.

I was confused as to why Mattie would want to play on a team where he was likely to be one of the lesser lights.

But having repeated what he said earlier, I pleaded and begged with him to reconsider but to no avail. 'We'll have a team in three years when the U14's come of age. We have many decent hurlers on that team. Sean Dunphy and Dara O Brien are starting for Dublin, Mattie King is going to be a great wing back and sure Conor Creaby could play at corner-back now.

'Mattie, even allowing for some human wastage from this bunch, we'll have a decent team then' I stressed.

The club had been instrumental with Ashbourne and Curragha GAA clubs in lobbying Ashbourne community college to start a hurling team for the first time. They eventually did, with no small part played by Sean Dunphy, who wouldn't take 'no' for an answer. Seven of that team were Wild Geese players. Inspired by these, Dara O'Brien took a leaf out that book and almost simultaneously his school St. Finians Community, Swords also started a hurling team for the first time with eight Geese players. These kids would soon be men and they where going to be good hurlers and inject the intensity we needed for lift off.

Still Mattie remained unconvinced.

'Mattie, you are a major part of that jigsaw. We'd hope to build the future team around the likes of you and Shane. At least sleep on it. You leaving could kill the team,' were my final words to him.

He promised me that he would.

I agreed not to talk to anyone about it for now. We both lied as it turned out. I was to discover that he had already signed the papers.

and as soon as Mattie had hung up I rang Flat's straight away.

'We're doomed, it's backwards from here,' was Flats's initial reply when I filled him in. We genuinely thought at this stage that he might change his mind.

If he did not, the big worry was how the others would take it, especially the senior players. It's not like we could replace him or them. Would the team survive? A feeling of betrayal came over me. He was putting himself before the team and the club. This was the first time we had faced this obstacle and what we did could have critical impact on hurling in the club.

Sean and I agreed to keep it under wraps for the moment, at least until Mattie called back.

Flats and I were on the ruling committee of the club and I knew if we wanted to block the transfer we could. But what were the pros and cons. If you object, you would have a disgruntled player or maybe he'd quit.

What effect would it have on the club and what message would it send out to the team and its supporters. Would it say we are lacking ambition?

I knew the strife it could cause. My father's home club, Tulsk Lords Edwards, were making a bit of a revival in the nineties, when their star player, Nigel Dineen, transferred to the club next door, Castlerea/St. Kevins.

Dineen went on to have a fine career as an inter-county player for over a decade and was the main driver in the Castlerea/St. Kevins team that won two senior county titles.

Dineen's house was the last house in the parish but my Uncle Joe, a devout Tulsk man, was not getting drawn on boundaries.

'He learned all his football with Tulsk, he has no business going to Castlerea' .

Joe said it had a 'devastating effect on the team and the club' for a long time.

Indeed that particular Tulsk team never recovered and instead of establishing themselves as a force in the senior ranks as they would have had Dineen stayed, they find themselves languishing between junior and intermediate levels today.

Interestingly enough, Dineen has two younger brothers, both decent footballers. One currently is on the Roscommon team and plays with Castlerea St.Kevins while his youngest brother, an U-21 Roscommon footballer, plays with Tulsk Lord Edwards.

Nigel's move led to much bitterness and regret and I was keen not to let that happen at Wild Geese. More importantly blocking Mattie's transfer might blight his progress as a hurler.

When Joan spent three months in Ballymaloe in 2009, Mikey and

I went down to visit her on several weekends. While there I often ventured to watch the local hurling team, Russell Rovers. They play Junior C in the Cork hurling championship. One player stood out, Brian Harnett. He played with his two brothers on the team, one of whom, Kevin, is a former Cork hurler. I was not surprised when I read Brian scored 1-14 in the Munster minor hurling championship in 2010 and made one of the Cork development squads. I was shocked when I read that he had handed in a transfer application in 2012 seeking a move to senior hurling neighbours Midleton. Russell Rovers objected, the county board went with the club as is the norm but Brian then refused to play for them and to make matters worse, so did his brothers. This made him ineligible for inter-county action under a Cork bye-law: But that same bye-law though makes him a free agent once he has not played for 96 weeks.

That's a hard call for a young hurler but I suppose if Russell Rovers were to let all their good players go, where would they be? Many of the locals see the clubs stance as proof of their ambition. I have heard since the two brothers have gone back playing for Rovers but the club will not change its mind on the objection to Brian's transfer and now he has lots of time on his hands. We were in a similar situation.

I had not heard from Mattie for a while but sure enough he called back the day before the Christmas party. Alas time had not softened his position and if anything he was more resolute than ever. I chose not to debate it this time and I just pleaded with him to come to the party.

He had been a good servant to our cause and deserved a proper send off. Even if most of the lads did not know it then, it was a 'last supper' of sorts.

I told him I had informed Flats and the only other people I'd told out of respect were the chairman, Ed and Peter. We'd keep it under wraps until after the party night. I did not want his career with us to end in bad terms.

After the night when the news had broken, some club members felt he had a cheek to come to the party. I wouldn't take no for an answer from him and was responsible for his appearance. Anyway, we had a good night and Mattie got player of the year, as voted by the other panellists.

The following day I rang the most senior players. My biggest fear was that there might be a domino effect. There were mixed responses. Shane was 'stunned', describing it as a 'disaster' while Peter was 'disappointed in him and disappointed for us.'

On the whole most of the panel took it well and while all were a bit taken a back, they were Dubs and there is a general acceptance here that this was the way things happen.

If the club had blocked the transfer it might have been more divisive but in the end it did not. If I was doing my job right I probably should have objected. If I had said to the chairman 'object' I'd say he would have.

I rang the county board. They said if we object they would back us on it and explained that if a guy tried to leave a smaller club to join a bigger club and the smaller club objects, the transfer would not go through.

While many on the clubs committee wanted to, myself and Flats persuaded them to allow it through and it was carried easily in the end.

One of the reasons that we allowed the transfer was on the basis that he had not come through the juvenile structure. But we were determined not to be caught a second time and as a result of Mattie's switch, we brought in an amendment to the club's constitution. This effectively torpedoed the prospect of any players from transferring out of the club if they had come through our juvenile channels.

It was agreed that if we did not protect the club, we would jeopardise our future and we might as well take the sign down and direct all interest to Swords.

JFK didn't play the game, although his Wexford ancestors did, and I reckon his famous saying is appropriate; 'ask not what your country can do for you but what you can do for your country'.

CHAPTER 20

NEAR DEATH, RESURRECTION AND THE LAND OF OZ

It's mid-January, Flats and I and the senior players meet for lunch. Those present are Mark, Philly, this years captain and vice captain respectively and Shane, who is still not working and was sleeping a lot. Not much else for him to do. Since mid-December nothing was moving in his line and little on the horizon. We are all still recovering from the wound of Mattie leaving us and needed reassurance. I wanted to take this opportunity to put our cards on the table, hear any suggestions, and avoid the pitfalls, which may have led to Mattie wanting to leave. I am a believer in changing things from the inside and from the beginning, have always encouraged the lads to be open and honest.

We know we are the lowest caste in hurling. We are not looking for a place in hurling's Valhalla but we do not want to be stuck around in Junior F for all our hurling lives.

Shane has been very quiet lately, although he spoke up and was involved in the planning for the upcoming season that day. He was more interested in 'what was for lunch' and I had the feeling something wasn't right, the sparkle was gone.

Was it the transfer? No I think it was gone before that. We discussed doing more training but the same old chestnuts reappeared. They were that lads were playing football twice weekly and then there were family commitments.

Many of the lads go to football training, knowing they'll be dropped if they do not turn up. The coaches can do that because of the big numbers. Hurling needs more practice but due to the lack of numbers, we could never tell lads 'if you do not train you'll not play'.

That's not just a Wild Geese issue but it's prevalent in all non-hurling heartlands. The only drastic change that resulted from the meeting, other then reconfirming our commitments for the year was that we'd quit training indoors because the numbers had got so small it was no longer economically viable.

At the first training session of the year, I talked a bit about Mattie leaving and pointed out while we where not happy with it, we now had to live with it and try not to let it dampen our spirit, plus Mattie was a mate and would always be. It was obvious that numbers were going to be an issue. For the first time in our existence we had a substantial longterm injury list. Chris Keane, Ed, Andy, Floody, Philly and Danny Monks where all injured. Danny Boxwell had gone back to college in Shannon and would now only be available some weekends.

I was struck when reading 'The Examiner' reviews of the Kerry County Championship at the scourge of emigration which had really bitten down there. For all our problems, we weren't that badly hit.

It was very sobering to read the amount of lads from just one county involved in senior football that had left these shores since the previous season.

Colm Doherty from Donnaghamore/Ashbourne GAA club was on looking for a challenge. Their club was a beneficiary of the 'Celtic Tiger'. Developers coveted their old grounds and in exchange they got three pitches and a massive club house with zero debt. The latter incorporated a stand, bar and indoor sports complex. I remember the first day we walked in there for a game, way back in 2008, we were told we were in 'dressing room 7 and pitch 2'. A different galaxy but Colm and his team have the same hurling struggles we have. That evening we were on Pitch 1, sand-based, floodlit field. We had a good turnout and got two new recruits into the bargain. One was Stephen O'Connor, a national schoolteacher from Enniscorthy, who had moved into the area and Mick Lally, a mate of Philly's from his St.Colmcilles football days. Both had played before but not for years.

Just before the game was due to start, our other national schoolteacher from Enniscorthy on the panel, Mick Kennedy approached me. We had not seen much of him as he had contracted pneumonia. 'Are ya not togging out?', I asked. 'Can I talk to you for a second,' he asked quietly back.

I nodded and stepped closer to him. He said:'I have cancer'.

I was speechless.

He told me after the pneumonia had gone, he had a further chest X-ray. The results aided by CAT scan showed a large mass in his right chest. The mass was pressing against some blood vessels to the brain. He paused before continuing: 'I remember my GP saying that the mass or tumour was the size of a sliotar. The GP referred me to the Mater Hospital and on 9th of February, I was told I had cancer'.

I just stood feeling helpless. 'God, Mick I am sorry to hear that, what's the prognosis?' I asked bluntly.

'I am going in next week, to start eight cycles of chemotherapy', he explained.

Still a bit numb and not from the -4 C night, I did not know what to say. 'How's Leah and the two girls holding up?' I asked.

They are good, thanks,' he replied.

Then Philly shouts over: 'Aidan, are we going to get this game going or what?'

'Mick, look you're a fighter and I know you'll beat this. If there is anything we can do please do not hesitate. I'll keep you in the loop and hopefully you'll be back to us soon,' and with that I ran into my starting position.

Life goes on but what a shock, it puts everything into perspective. What Mick had said was still going around in my head. A sound lad, a very dedicated and reliable member of the team, he was going to be a loss but the bigger picture was about his survival.

Game on, for the first 15 minutes that night, it looked like our star had risen, we resembled Kilkenny but eventually we settled back into our old selves losing 4-4 to 0-12 with soft goals again proving our undoing.

We never laid eyes on Philly's mate again and it was not from the lack of encouragement. Stephen O'Connor on the other hand, was keen and handy but rusty. You could see the potential. It was a weird coincidence, the day Mick broke the news a new Enniscorthy lad arrived. While both are national schoolteachers they did not know each other. Our first two league games clashed with cup football and thus we struggled to even field a team. When the clocks change to summer time, the two codes rarely clash but for the few games before that, it can be a nightmare and as a result we could be out of a competition before it's hardly started.

We lost the first fixture narrowly. That day we experimented by playing Shane Byrne at centre-forward but it didn't work. For our next game away to Clontarf he just never turned up. We have all heard of the Battle of Clontarf, well that day was a massacre and the furthest we had ever been from the Promised Land, if there is such a place for us. Everything that could go wrong went wrong. The unseasonably hot March weather had thousands flocking to the seafront and we got caught up in traffic. As a result we arrived late. Most of the lads available had played football earlier and were knackered. We had 15 but Clontarf had only 13, so we played 13 a side. After a few minutes it was obvious that most of their 13 were off the first team by the standard of their play. Hurling artistry at its best. We had beaten them by two points in the corresponding game the previous October but this team were vastly superior. The final score was 9-21 to 1-5. It was the lowest point since we had started the journey. I was the last to leave the dressing-room, while I knew the score was a lie and the fact that they gave us a walk over when our championship fixture came around later in the season confirmed this. The situation with Shane, the absence of the injured, the game clashing with other sports, it all was beginning to wear me down.

I felt like Don Quixote's mule! At least that clown had windmills to tilt at! And a sense of purpose.

Shane had previously spoken about the lack of intensity at the training but instead of urging the lads forward he walked away because his heart was no longer in it.

He just could not give 100 per cent commitment to both sports and soccer won out. He was not prepared to slog it out at Junior F any more.

When Joe Deane first played for Cork, the first of 50 appearances, he was playing junior hurling with Killeagh. The locals will tell you he single-handedly dragged them over a decade to the senior levels of Cork hurling. Losing our two top players was an almighty blow but was it their fault?

Or was it us?

Maybe it was a bit of both. I recall one game where we played St. Sylvesters in 2010 and they beat us by 2-12 to 1-8. I came into the dressing-room afterwards and I was delighted because we had played very well and up the last 10 or 15 minutes we were in with a chance.

We had performed very well. We gave them a good fright but the reality is they were better than us, they were younger than us and they had played a lot longer than us.

But he could never understand why I came into the dressing-room so happy and I think now he feels he's playing with a team that doesn't tick his boxes any more. I knew we had to crawl before we could walk let alone sprint.

For me it was a time of reflection. This was definitely our nadir. No matter what spin we put on it, the immediate future of the adult team seemed very uncertain. When I spoke to Sean about it he was equally despondent. You can only go against the tide for so long.

Victor Hugo put it; 'even the darkest night will end and the sun will rise' and it did that April, the club had organised in association with the Co. Board a new GPO to help train the juveniles, Stephen O'Meara. It's amazing how life can come around full circle. Stephen, a close friend of John Rennie's had been coached two decades before by Ed. He took the U15s under his wing and with Sean Flatley brought them up to the next level very fast. We trained the same night and same time to allow the use of the pitch at 7.30 for the clubs newly formed ladies team. So by default we ended up merging with the U15s to train. The sessions under Stephen were intensive and vibrant. It helped having 25 to 30 there most nights with the bulk being under-15.

Our lads could now see a good future for the team. Sean and I warned all the adults to take it easy if they came into contact with the juveniles when playing and Stephen structured the training games in a way that we'd not cross swords much. We did not want this new arrangement to backfire.

Out of the blue we got a bunch of new players. Our biggest influx since the heydays of 2008. Sean Bond and his brother Michael joined. Sean had played years before with Fingallians but his brother was new to the game. Tom Smyth also persuaded his brother Eoin to join. Eoin also known as 'Slim' had never played before. A big bearded lad, weighting in at 14.5 stone, he resembled one of the bearded trio that won an All-Ireland with Tyrone in 2008. It was not long before he caught the hurling bug. Another Starlights player, David Donohue, a cousin of the Kealy brothers and new resident to the village, Jarlath Kingston also arrived on the same evening.

In an all too familiar tune, both had played years before and were eager to take up where they left off. In another bizarre twist my best friend Martin Nulty called to say that his new apprentice horticulturalist, a Spanish lad, wanted to play hurling, could I accommodate him?

At first I was sceptical. A 19-year-old Spaniard. I know we were stuck, at first I thought Martin was having me on but he persisted. Fortunately as it turned out. When the lad first appeared in Oldtown, I brought him over to the side of the pitch to see if he could play. I did not want his blood on my hands but I was instantly amazed at how he handled the hurl, a natural, if there can be such a thing!

Oriol Hally-Garcia, standing at 5'9, certainly looks like the quintessential Spaniard, dark and tanned but he spoke perfect English (with a Laois accent). When I introduced him to the lads, he filled us in on his family history. He was seven when his family emigrated to Barcelona from Dublin. His father had played hurling before for Laois and Oriol had inherited his Dad's hurling DNA. Oriol's twin brother, who he said looks more Irish, also has an unusual past-time, 'human castelling', where people stand on each other to make towers in Spain.

'No fear of that catching on here, with this country's obesity problem' says Philly.

Even with the same long injury list, selection was suddenly going to become tricky.

The same month, Mick Kennedy texted me with great news – he had a treatable cancer. He said all was going well and that he expected to be back with us by the autumn.

I told the lads and they were jubilant. That April the Ashbourne Community School hurling team got to a Leinster hurling final while the St. Finians hurling team got to a Dublin schools final. Both lost but were powered by Wild Geese hurlers. The hurling seed had not fallen on barren ground. We had an exciting future. We won our next two league matches. With Oriol and Nathan at midfield, we had two engines that would not be out of place on a senior team. I was looking forward to the championship.

Unfortunately the group stages of that turned into a bit of a farce. We were in a group of eight, with the top four qualifying for a quarter-final. Our aim was top two as that secured a home game, that's something we'd never achieved before. After the first five fixtures we sat on top with full points but had scored zero and conceded zero. Yes five walk over's. Five super clubs were unable to field teams and then pulled out at the last minute. So our first championship game came on the 19th of July against Naomh Barrog, who had hammered us the previous year. That evening we were so wound up we could not spring. We matched them from the start and were unlucky to be 1-3 to 0-4 down at half-time. Stephen O'Meara who now took us under his wing, gave an enlightened interval talk and we made the necessary tactical changes. Some times it takes a fresh set of eyes to see things that those involved overlook.

Stephen is not a traditionalist, a former O'Toole's player who has played at the highest level. He now asks us to break with tradition. 'Lads I know ground hurling is gospel but it's a waste of time, you might win the pull but then you are most likely to lose possession. Get it into your hands. If you have it, they do not. If they do not have it, you're in the driving seat.'

We listened to this fresh voice and realised it made sense, especially at our level. He finished with 'lads please do not forget, put both hands on the hurl when taking up the ball, do the simple thing right and you can win'.

Philly who was playing at centre-back thundered over a long range effort to kickstart our comeback. All was going well until Dave Rennie had to go off injured. Dave is doing a retail management degree. Paid for by Lidl, he does 16 weeks in college and then 16 weeks in the store but thankfully it was his left and not his writing arm and that this injury coincides with his college time thus not affecting his work.

Naomh Barrog pulled ahead and although Sean Madigan goaled for us near the climax, we ended up losing by four points. But it was a good performance, we were upbeat and we looked forward to the visit of Parnell's the following Monday night for our final championship group game.

It was a warm wet Monday night. What a summer it had been. Rainfall levels for June broke all the records and July was following a similar pattern. Paul Kealy was smiling from ear to ear that evening. 'God you're in great form,' says Slim, who is now part of the furniture, as Paul walked into the dressing-room.

'I sure am, just got news in work that I am being made permanent' Paul replied. After some back-slapping and more immature jokes about the pill, we settled down and named the team.

I warned the lads about giving away soft frees especially on the wet ground and also stressed that whatever the ref said we agreed with. I was looking at John Rennie for that one. I finished with: 'Lads go in good and hard but no dirty play'.

As Peter was working, Stephen O'Meara took control of the line for us. He talked tactics for a few minutes, we took to the field, completed a short warm-up and then went on-air. Stephen O'Connor and David Donohue gave us the perfect start with two fine points. Philly at centre-back was brilliant and breaking up most of their attacks. Stephen on the line was at him the whole time not to venture forward 'stay in your position and do what you do best' he hollered.

A long 'Hail Mary' effort from Tom Smyth was going wide until John Rennie managed to tap it across the box where I was on hand to bury it. Rennie himself got a second and we lead 2-5 to 0-5 at the break. It was clear to us now, avoiding ground hurling was helping. Within 10 minutes of the restart we had two more goals and were cruising. Nathan and Oriol at midfield, one faster then the other were everywhere and everything was going like clockwork until one of their lads hit Oriol off the ball. The referee spotted it and issued red. Having an extra-man disjointed us massively. It was the second time in three games that our performance suffered as a result of being a man up. Parnell's staged a comeback but we held on to win 4-7 to 3-5 and secure for the first time in our history a home quarter-final berth. The dressing-room was a happy place that evening.

Our next league game was a formidable one, away to St. Sylvesters, as they sit second in the table and were looking good for promotion. By now, mid-August, the work for Oriol had dried up and he was back in Barcelona. If we were going to win the championship, we figured it would only be with him, so we agreed to up the referee expenses money to €5 each for the Sylvesters game and use the difference to get him over for the quarter-final. A few days before the game, I got a call from Sean Madigan. 'I have good news and bad news for you' he declared.

'Okay Sean, give us the bad news first,' I replied.

'I am going to have to retire from the hurling,' he said.

'So what's the good news?' I asked.

'I'm emigrating to Australia.'

'You're kidding,' I replied.

'I'm not. I'm off in a few weeks, job lined up, visa secured,' he assured me.

'What about Barbara and the kids?' I interjected.

'I'll be back in December for the brother's wedding, by then I'll have a home sorted in Oz, school places got. Then me, Barbara and the four kids will head down under for good in January.'

This was unexpected, Sean lived, worked, socialised and in fact did everything within a few hundred metres from his home place in St. Margarets.

'What's brought this about?' I asked.

'Look,' he went on, 'there is not much happening here at the moment in the line of work but the main reason is I lived there before, loved it and I reckon for Barbara and the kids it's an offer of a better way of life. Ireland is not what it used to be.'

While Sean is no spring chicken, I could tell by the sound of his voice that he was happy he was doing the right thing for him and his family. He is now and will always be young at heart. Fair play to him, this is his dream and he's going for it.

In the dressing-room after training the following evening, I was relaying the news to the lads, when lightening struck again. Sean McNulty told us that he had just heard Gerry Fitzsimons is going down the yellowbrick road as well, in September.

I had only got to know him after we formed the adult team. Gerry is the ideal non-playing club man. Over the past three years he had been the catalyst for an extension of the dressing-rooms, upgrading the showers and through his building contacts obtained a port cabin for the club for free. The second I met him in 2008, we hit if off. While he's from Ballymun, long before it was built up, he spent many of his teenage summers visiting with his aunt and uncle in the west. His uncle, a garda sergeant was the previous occupier of the garda barracks in Kiltormer before we moved in there in July 1980. Gerry had spent many of his summer holidays in the same tiny east Galway village that I grew up in.

That was a nice coincidence. I rang him when I got home. He said he got a job offer in Perth he could not refuse and was off shortly. The same friend that got him the job, he had soldiered with in San Francisco in the eighties, during Ireland's last bad run. That friend had never come home and had made good in Perth. It was with a heavy heart he filled me in on the details. His wife and family were not being uprooted. His intention was to come home frequently. Gerry is a builder in the true fashion of the word, he had worked hard, never gone nuts like many in his industry but confessed 'the last two years have been brutal, I battled and managed to survive but it's a war I cannot win. So I am winding down the company and taking this opportunity while I can'.

He felt at 45 he could grasp this chance but if he waited any longer, it might be too late. Unlike Sean Madigan he was not happy about it but felt he had no choice. For the few days after, I was angry. Not with the lads but with the choices they had to make. The spectre of emigration that has haunted the island for hundreds of year was hanging over us again like a grim reaper. My generation, the 'because your worth it' generation, was guilty of cooking the golden goose and the future looks very bleak. To lose two men like that was a massive blow. Both were very community-minded and wore the club on their sleeve – always. The land of Oz is certainly going to be the richer from their presence.

I had snapped out of it by Sunday. We beat St. Sylvester's 1-9 to 0 -10, the difference was a scuttery goal from Tom Kennedy. He received the pass for the all-important score from Fionn Andrews, Val's youngest son, a hurling fanatic, who was making his debut. While the management of the adult team had made the decision not to rush the current U15s too fast into the adult ranks, Fionn was different. He was marginally too old to play with them and now had just turned 16. His arrival heralded as Churchill put it 'not the beginning of the end but the end of the beginning'.

And what of the future. A lot of those young people that are coming through are from Oldtown and Rolestown and are actually living in the area and for them there will be much more of a sense of pride.

Not as much with the current group. But if you are playing with your local parish it means more to you.

Most of their postal addresses will be Oldtown or Rolestown. I honestly think the future is very secure from that point of view.

And that's why this year has been a bit of a nightmare in terms of keeping things ticking over. We will not rush through the U15 in dribs and drabs. No, the ideal solution is to have them all come through at the same time when they are 18, which means we must survive for a few more years.

PS I met Shane at his brothers 40th party and he said he'll be back with us next season. He misses the camaraderie and the feeling of the hurl in his hand. Good man Shane. Sure we never doubted you.

LIST OF THOSE WHO PLAYED HURLING
WITH US BETWEEN 2008 AND 2012

AIDAN SKAHILL	FIONN ANDREWS	NIALL FINNEGAN
AIDAN LENEHAN	GAVIN DUNGAN	NOEL MOONEY
ARRON CREIGHON	GEORGE BLAINE	ORIOL HALLY-GARCIA
ANDY RYAN	GRAHAM MOORE	PADDY JONES
ANTHONY GAFFNEY	GREG RALPH	PAUL FLOOD
BRIAN O'NEILL	JARLATH KINGSTON	PAUL KEALY
CHARLIE ROONEY	JAMES BROWNE	PAUL LUMLEY
CHRIS KEANE	JAMES REILLY	PETER DUNPHY
CIARAN SMITH	JAMIE SUTTON	PETER McGOWAN
COLIN PRENDERVILLE	JASON SMITH	PETER SLYE
COLM DOHERTY	JOEY O'RIAN	PHILIP EGAN
DAMIEN KIELY	JORDAN GILCHRIST	PHILIP McCARTHY
DANNY BOXWELL	JOHN BARRETT	RICHARD DALY
DANNY KELLY	JOHN RENNIE	RICHIE MONKS
DANNY MITCHELL	KEITH McLOUGHLIN	SEAN BOND
DANNY MONKS	KEITH CHAPMAN	SEAN FLATLEY
DARYL BROWNE	KEVIN CONWAY	SEAN MADIGAN
DAVE RENNIE	KEVIN MONKS	SHANE BYRNE
DAVID DONOHUE	LUKE GRIFFEN	SIMON MADDEN
DAVID DOWD	MATTIE LAMBE	STEPHEN MAHER
DAVID GREEN	MARK KEALY	STEPHEN O'CONNOR
DAVID McDONALD	MARK McCAFFREY	STEPHEN O'MEARA
DAVID REILLY	MARTIN LEE	STEPHEN BARRETT
DAVIN BROWNE	MARTIN FLANAGAN	STEVE RYAN
DERRICK DALY	MICK KENNEDY	TOM DRAPER
ED SWEETMAN	MICK LALLY	TOM KENNEDY
EOIN SMYTH	MICK CONNELL	TOM SMYTH
EOIN McPHILBIN	MICHAEL BOND	
FIAC ANDREWS	NATHAN McCAFFREY	

RESULTS

2008 RECORD

Played 23　　**Won** 1　　**Draw** 1　　**Lost** 21

Junior E Championship

Setanta	1-9	Wild Geese	1-9
Wild Geese	1-10	St. Joseph's/O'Connell Boys	2-11
Kilmacud Crokes	3-12	Wild Geese	2-8
St.Peregrines	4-3	Wild Geese	2-1
Wild Geese	0-9	Parnells	2-13

Adult Hurling League 7

Kevins	3 – 17	Wild Geese	0-6
Wild Geese	0-4	St.Brendans	3-5
Wild Geese	0-4	Ballinteer St.Johns	3-17

Hurling Cup

Wild Geese	1-6	Raheny	5-7

Challenges

Played 14　　**Won** 1　　**Draw** 0　　**Lost** 13

2009 RECORD

Played 30　　**Won** 14　　**Draw** 4　　**Lost** 12

Junior E Championship

Setanta	2-6	Wild Geese	0-8
Wild Geese	0-12	Civil Service	0-3
Kilmacud Crokes	1-7	Wild Geese	3-6
Wild Geese	0-17	Na Fianna	0-10
Commercials	4-7	Wild Geese	1-11

Quarter-final

St. Pats Palmerstown	4-6	Wild Geese	1-10

Adult Hurling League 8

Clontarf	5-8	Wild Geese	2-4
Wild Geese	3-5	Erin Go Bragh	1-4
Wild Geese	1-8	Raheny	1-5
Kilmacud Crokes	0-13	Wild Geese	3-6
Civil Service	4-6	Wild Geese	2-8
Wild Geese	w/o	St. Peregrines	scr
Na Fianna	scr	Wild Geese	w/o
Wild Geese	w/o	St. Josephs/OCB	scr
Wild Geese	w/o	Commercials	scr
Wild Geese	2-12	Whitehall Colmcilles	2-12
Setanta	2-5	Wild Geese	2-7

League Final

Setanta	1-2	Wild Geese	2-6

Hurling Cup

Wild Geese	1-8	Erin Go Bragh	1-8
Wild Geese	2-8	Setanta	1-12
Whitehall Colmcilles	2-9	Wild Geese	2-9
Na Fianna	0-10	Wild Geese	2-5
Wild Geese	0-16	Kilmacud Crokes	0-12
Wild Geese	0-11	Civil Service	0-11

Leinster League Cup

Greystones (Wicklow)	2-14	Wild Geese	0-5
Wild Geese	1-5	St. Feckins (Louth)	2-10

Challenges

Played 8   **Won** 4   **Draw** 0   **Lost** 4

2010 RECORD

Played 30   **Won** 9   **Draw** 1   **Lost** 20

Junior E Championship

St. Peregrines	0-4	Wild Geese	3-14
Wild Geese	w/o	St. Josephs/OCB	scr
Setanta	1-11	Wild Geese	0-5
Civil Service	3-6	Wild Geese	1-3
Wild Geese	3-3	St. Pats Palmerstown	2-8

Quarter-final

| Skerries | 3-19 | Wild Geese | 0-4 |

Adult Hurling League 7

Wild Geese	0-7	Whitehall Colmcilles	2-11
Skerries	2-10	Wild Geese	0-9
Parnells	1-13	Wild Geese	0-9
Wild Geese	w/o	Clan Na Gael	scr
SOP/ER	4-16	Wild Geese	1-4
Wild Geese	1-9	St. Sylvesters	2-12
Thomas Davis	2-13	Wild Geese	0-8
Wild Geese	0-4	Erins Isle	3-14
Crumlin	4-10	Wild Geese	2-9
Wild Geese	1-4	St. Judes	3-14
Wild Geese	0-13	Setanta	1-10

Hurling Cup

| Na Fianna | 2-14 | Wild Geese | 2-5 |
| Civil Service | 2-14 | Wild Geese | 4-10 |

Challenges

Played 13   **Won** 7   **Draw** 0   **Lost** 6

2011 RECORD

Played 30   **Won** 7   **Draw** 3   **Lost** 20

Junior F Championship

Wild Geese	2-8	Good Counsel	0-6
Nh. Barrog	1-13	Wild Geese	1-4
Wild Geese	2-5	SOP/ER	0-2
St. Marks	3-12	Wild Geese	1-5
Wild Geese	1-13	Parnells	1-3
St. Josephs/OCB	3-7	Wild Geese	3-6

Quarter-final

Lucan Sarsfields	1-10	Wild Geese	2-6

Adult Hurling League 9

Wild Geese	3-13	St. Josephs/OCB	2-8
Whitehall Colmcilles	2-8	Wild Geese	2-8
Wild Geese	1-15	St. Peregrines	3-9
Lucan Sarsfields	3-9	Wild Geese	1-6
Wild Geese	1-10	St. Pats Donabate	3-6
Realt Dearg	0-10	Wild Geese	1-13
Wild Geese	1-11	Good Counsel	2-10
Wild Geese	3-7	Clontarf	1-11
Wild Geese	2-9	SOP/ER	1-13
Nh. Mearnog	2-8	Wild Geese	1-5
Erin Go Bragh	2-6	Wild Geese	0-15

Challenges

Played 12   **Won** 0   **Draw** 1   **Lost** 11

2012 RECORD (up to the end of September)
Played 21   **Won** 8   **Draw** 0   **Lost** 13

Junior F Championship

Wild Geese	w/o	Ballinteer St. Johns	scr
Nh. Olaf	scr	Wild Geese	w/o
Wild Geese	w/o	Clontarf	scr
Na Fianna	scr	Wild Geese	w/o
Whitehall Colmcilles	scr	Wild Geese	w/o
Wild Geese	1-8	Nh. Barrog	1-14
Wild Geese	4-7	Parnells	3-5

Quarter-final

Wild Geese	0-8	Crumlin	3-5

Adult Hurling League 9

Wild Geese	0-6	Realt Dearg	1-11
Clontarf	9-21	Wild Geese	1-5
Wild Geese	2-8	St. Peregrines	1-6
Wild Geese	1-10	Raheny	0-8
Good Counsel	3-6	Wild Geese	3-4
Wild Geese	2-9	Lucan Sarsfields	2-10
St. Sylvesters	0-10	Wild Geese	1-9

Challenges
Played 11   **Won** 4   **Draw** 0   **Lost** 7